Mark Wallington had a variety of jobs before embarking as a TV scriptwriter and a travel writer. He worked in a pork pie factory, on a Sardinian building site, in a lumbermill, as a gardener and for a bicycle messenger service in San Francisco.

As a travel writer Mark Wallington is the author of *Destination Lapland* and *500 Mile Walkies,* and a freelance contributor to a variety of publications. His hobbies include playing the guitar in the bathroom and watching Grandstand.

D0524320

Boogie up the River

One Man and his Dog to the Source of the Thames

Mark Wallington

ARROW BOOKS

Arrow Books Limited
20 Vauxhall Bridge Road, London SW1V 2SA

An imprint of Random Century Group

London Melbourne Sydney Auckland
Johannesburg and agencies throughout
the world

First published in Great Britain by Hutchinson 1989
Arrow edition 1990

© Mark Wallington 1989

Printed and bound in Great Britain by
Courier International Ltd, Tiptree, Essex

ISBN 0 09 965910 7

For Catherine

Contents

1. I'll See You on Tower Pier at Eleven

I made a lot of phone calls that evening. It was the eve of departure and I was getting desperate.

I was standing at the window with the receiver pressed to my ear and I remember thinking how the clouds were wound around the brown sky like a river. But everywhere I looked I saw a river. I had rivers on my mind.

I rang my friend Douglas. I told him I was about to set off on a long journey, a journey by boat to the source of a great river, a journey to the source of the Thames. And he said: 'So what; doesn't impress me.'

So I went straight to the point. I said: 'I want you to do me a favour. I want you to look after Boogie.'

It was a reasonable request. I had after all looked after his stick insects when he went windsurfing in Turkey.

He said: 'Boogie?'

'Yes.'

'Your dog?'

'Yes.'

'The dog that ate my stick insects when I went windsurfing in Turkey?'

I didn't pursue the matter. Douglas clearly has a better memory than I have. Instead I phoned Clive. I explained to Clive that I was about to row to the source of the

Thames, that I was setting off in the morning and that
my craft would be an antique camping skiff, and he said:
'Big deal! I've just come back from a desert safari in
Tunisia.'

'I was wondering if Boogie could stay with you while
I'm gone,' I said.

There was silence, then Clive said: 'Boogie?'

'My dog.'

'The dog you brought round here once?'

'That's right.'

'The dog that ate my computer?'

Actually that's not true. It was Clive's computer soft-
ware Boogie ate rather than the computer itself. I didn't
pursue the matter though, instead I phoned Sarah. But
Sarah said she couldn't look after Boogie either. She said
she was going to South America on business. This surprised me since she works behind the counter at Sketchley's, but I wished her a pleasant trip and then phoned
Kevin. Kevin is an old friend. Kevin has a dog of his own.
Kevin had even looked after Boogie once before. But
when Kevin answered he reminded me of the stain on his
ceiling, the enormous phone bill, the dent in his Vauxhall
Astra, and the paternity suit filed against his own dog, all
consequences, he claimed, of Boogie's visit. I thought the
man was over-reacting, personally, but I didn't pursue the
matter.

I went through my address book once more. Marsha
was my last chance. As I dialled, Boogie came into the
room to watch the new Australian mini-series on TV. He
glanced at me. It was a glance that said: 'Here, you know
that new frying pan?'

'Yes.'

'The Teflon job?'

'Yes.'

'I've just been sick in it.'

Marsha answered. I felt confident Marsha would help me out. Marsha loves all animals. She particularly likes monkeys. In fact she's monkey crazy. She has monkey-pattern wallpaper. If you visit her and she gives you a cup of tea the chances are the cup will have a gibbon on it. Marsha also likes dogs and so I said to her: 'Marsha. I'm going on a rowing trip up the Thames. I'm going to solve the mystery of its source once and for all. I'll be going uphill for a hundred and forty miles on a journey through the wilds of the stockbroker belt.'

And she said: 'You should take a chimpanzee with you.'

So I explained how I didn't want to take any animal with me and that the reason I was phoning was because . . .

'You're not going to ask me to look after Boogie, are you?'

'Yes.'

'Boogie, your dog? The dog that came round here once?'

I could vaguely remember taking Boogie round to her house once before. She gave him a bowl of water; I think the bowl had a gorilla on it. 'You remember him,' I said.

'How could I forget him? He tried to seduce my hamster.'

I didn't pursue the matter. I put the phone down and patted Boogie. He belched, and a miasma of curry and Winalot wound around the room like a river. I could never understand what all the fuss was about. He was charmingly noisome, that was all. Beneath his earthy exterior was an honest animal simply trying to unload his traumatic childhood. All he wanted was to be understood. Normally I took him with me on trips like this, but that was out of the question this time. This time Jennifer was coming with me.

Outside the daylight was stretched. It was the beginning

of May, the time of year when you begin to forget that the days were ever short, and I could feel the mounting excitement of an imminent journey.

I made one last effort: I called Mrs Matheson.

'Hello,' said Mrs Matheson. 'Sit And Stay Boarding Kennels.'

'Hello, this is Mark Wallington.'

'We're full!'

The problem is Boogie has a reputation on the kennel circuit. He's known as a bad influence on the other guests. He's like Bilko in kennels – he organizes poker schools and plans escapes. The last time he stayed with Mrs Matheson even the other dogs complained.

'But you're my only hope, Mrs Matheson. I've tried everywhere else. I'm going away tomorrow.'

'We're full until Christmas.'

'I'd take him with me but I'm going with a friend and . . . well . . . she hates him.'

'And I've just remembered we're full until the following Christmas as well.'

'It'll be a disaster if he comes with us. Couldn't you keep him in the fridge or something?'

'In fact I really don't think we can fit him in this century.'

Before I could pursue the matter she hung up.

On the Australian mini-series the heroine stood in the shade of a gum tree and told the hero she loved him and Boogie licked his armpit. Hadn't I heard stories of how cat owners went away for a week and left their cats seven tins of cat food in a row?

Boogie looked at me and grinned. He's the only dog I know who has a can opener attached to his collar.

There was nothing else I could do. Jennifer would just have to grow to like him; she'd have to make an effort. I called her and spoke to her answering machine.

'Hello, it's Mark . . . um . . . I just called to tell you . . . well . . . just to say . . . to say about tomorrow . . . nothing really . . . just meet me at Tower Pier at eleven . . . and . . . well, see you there.'

I couldn't tell her over the phone. Informing someone that they're going to spend a lengthy period in an enclosed space with Boogie should be done to the face. She'd find out tomorrow and then it would be her problem.

I packed nervously. As I zipped up my bag Boogie came over and gave me his 'going somewhere, are you?' look. I sighed, unzipped the bag and squeezed in his bowl. He wagged his tail and knocked over an inexpensive ornament that didn't break, then gave me his 'and you simply couldn't bear to leave me behind, could you?' look.

Then we sat down and watched the end of the mini-series. But I couldn't concentrate. I kept seeing rivers everywhere.

2. All Right, The Prospect of Whitby at Eight

A journey to the source of the Thames wasn't my idea; it was Jennifer's. Not that I'm holding her responsible for what happened – that would be unreasonable, there were far too many people involved to blame one individual. Even the manager of my local branch of The Sock Shop played a part. If he hadn't arranged his window the way he did that evening back in March things might have been very different.

I remember the occasion well. I was on my way round to Jennifer's flat in Docklands. We get together now and again. We have poetry evenings. She reads me her poems and asks for comment. She says I'm the only person she could possibly do this with. She says I'm different from her other friends. She says they all have Porsches and cufflinks, while I have sensitivity. They live on their stock market knowledge and their nerves, while I live on a whim.

I don't know where she gets this idea from but I'm certainly not going to discourage her. If anything I try to cultivate the image. I stare out of windows a lot when I'm with her. I appear preoccupied, as if I'm hiding something. I dress plainly on the surface but like an El Greco underneath. For this reason when I saw the green and yellow viscose creations in The Sock Shop window, I thought: Those socks talk. Quite what they said I wasn't sure, but Jennifer is a woman who likes to be kept guessing. She said to me once: 'The two things in life I love most are poetry and money.' She's an enigma, a contradiction; it's just a shame her poetry is so dreadful.

I changed in the lift on the way up to her apartment. It was the first time I'd ever been to a poetry evening with a dirty pair of socks in my pocket. I sat on the floor as she read me her latest work. When Jennifer reads poetry she lets her hair down and then spends the evening throwing it back off her face. She takes her shoes off and sits cross-legged and tries to sell me the poem as if it were gilt-edged stock. It's most effective.

' "Rubble lies like flesh in the streets, and my mind wanders picking at the bones . . ." ' she read, and then she stopped and pouted and said: 'It's awful, isn't it?'

'No . . . no . . . it's . . . promising, definitely promising,' I said, and then the telephone rang.

I went to the window and gazed out over London. Jennifer's flat is in one of the development schemes that rise every week from the mess that was once Wapping. She doesn't say much about her past but I have a feeling she's known the Docklands since she was a child. A lot of her poems are based around them – the word rubble has appeared more than once. She bought the flat for the price of the bricks and now if she sold it she could buy a Lincolnshire market town. She says she doesn't think about it. She means she doesn't like to think about it.

Across the river among the warehouses the new silver buildings reached for the sky like fresh tombstones. In the street below, an Audi Quattro rumbled over the cobblestones past a line of builders' skips and estate agents' offices.

I kicked my own shoes off and my socks hit the white

carpet like a spilt drink. But the shag-pile poked through the viscose and irritated my feet and when Jennifer came off the telephone I said: 'I've got really itchy feet.'

She smiled and her big eyes widened and slipped into that faraway look she has and she said: 'You're not planning another trip, are you?'

'What . . . ?'

'That's what I like about you. Nobody owns you. You look out of a window, become inspired and off you go. What far-flung corner are you heading to this time?'

The problem with Jennifer is that she likes to charm people but doesn't like much to be charmed herself. When she gives you her faraway look she threads your eyes and she takes control like a puppeteer. She makes you feel you are the only person who really matters. She even makes you forget about the other ten people she has made feel exactly the same way already that day, and I knew I would never be able to forgive myself if I admitted that when I mentioned itchy feet I was commenting on my new socks rather my wanderlust, so I said: 'Well . . .'

On a pier a police boat gargled into life. On the bank I was sure another slim building had appeared since I last looked. Through it all rolled the mighty Thames.

'. . . I think it's about time I went on a journey to the source of a great river.'

This wasn't altogether untrue. Every spring I think about going to the source of a great river, or the top of a great mountain, or across a great ocean, or to the heart of a great continent. I spend the winter locked in the den of my body. I leave the curtains drawn and windows closed and I eat things out of packets. Then the clocks go forward and I'm struck down by impatience. I pull out atlases and I read books like Charles Sturt's *Narrative of an Expedition into Central Australia*. I listen to the shipping forecast. I throw open the windows and see the blossom and I take deep breaths and say things like: 'I think it's about time I went on a trip to the source of a great river.'

Normally I'm on my own when I behave like this, and within a few days it's all forgotten and there's no damage done. But this time I was with Jennifer, and Jennifer has this idea I'm the last of the great adventurers. She's excited by the thought of me swinging through trees to get a story. She doesn't realize I spend most of my life sitting in my attic looking out over the gas showroom. I keep meaning to tell her but whenever I'm on the verge she says: 'Why don't I just pack up all this work business and go on an adventure with you?' and I'm helpless. On this particular occasion she stared downstream towards Millwall and said: 'I'd love to go to the source of a great river as well.' And I panicked and replied: 'Name your river and we'll travel together to its source.'

I quickly followed this with a nervous laugh in the hope she'd think twice before committing herself to a raft on the Orinoco with a nautical buffoon. But she just stood there watching a balloon bearing the name of a building society fly over the water. I could see the globe in her eyes. I could see the word Amazon on her lips. Then she turned to me and said: 'The Thames.'

'The what?'

'The Thames.'

'The Thames.'

'Yes. The Thames.'

'You mean . . . The Thames?'

'Yes. The Thames.'

'Let me get this right. You want to go . . . to the source of the Thames?'

'Yes.'

'Why?'

'Because it's here.'

'You mean because it's there. The phrase is: because it's there.'

'No, because it's here. Because it's here, right outside my window.'

'Oh.'

The rest of the evening we dedicated to Thames poetry: ' "Sweete Themmes! runne softlie, till I end my Song," ' read Jennifer from the Spenser collection. ' "Earth has not anything to show more fair," ' read I from the Wordsworth. Later she dug into a drawer and read me one of her own poems about the river. She stroked her hair back and said: ' "When I lie on your bed I see greyness and strange stains. When I lie on your surface, I just see greyness, I'm sinking into . . ." It's awful, isn't it?'

'No, no. it's . . . promising,' I said, and then the phone went again.

It wasn't until I drove home and found myself driving along the Thames Embankment that I began to think seriously of what she'd said. By Blackfriars Bridge I parked and peered into the black and gold water and I felt I was looking at the river for the first time. As it rolled through the city I could sense the power of an enormous history, and I began to understand Jennifer's distraction. The Thames *is* here rather than there. The Thames is our river – Britain's river. The Thames coils like an intestine through the belly of the nation. A voyage to its source would be an important journey.

So I began to make casual inquiries. Popular opinion had it that the source of the Thames was near Cirencester in Gloucestershire. But then I met a man in a pub who said: 'Bollocks!' and went on to explain that the source was undoubtedly at Seven Springs near Cheltenham. I passed this information on to the woman in the library and she said: 'The source of the Thames? It's in Crudwell, everyone knows that.' Then I brought the subject up at a dinner party and was amazed at the silence it inspired. And so I began to wonder: had I stumbled across a geographical riddle? Could a river as well charted as the Thames really have a disputed source? It didn't seem credible. I intensified my research and consulted my AA atlas of Great Britain. I followed the course of the river as it wound out of London as blue as a motorway, headed on through Berkshire and the Goring Gap, and turned north to Oxford. As far as there it was a regular ribbon of water but then as it set out through open country it gave the first signs of the strange behaviour to come. It took to wandering drunkenly through nowhere in particular. Somewhere it slipped unnoticed into Gloucestershire, and passed Lechlade as if it were lost. Finally it reached Cricklade and there things got out of control, as, without warning, the river split into a frayed end and veins ran off like leaks from a pipe. It seemed to me that any one of these could have been the source. I put my maps down and wiped a tear from my eye. It was time, I decided, that someone settled the dispute once and for all.

A fortnight later I saw Jennifer again. We arranged to meet in the Prospect of Whitby in Docklands. She was forty-five minutes late. I watched her as she parked her TVR outside and snarled at a youth who leant against a lamp post. As she crossed the road to the pub a vagrant shuffled towards her and asked her for money. She gave him ten pounds and kissed his head.

In the pub we sat underneath a photograph of Dennis Waterman and George Cole being pally with the landlord. Since I'd last seen her Jennifer had been to Munich once, Bologna twice, and had had lunch with Adam Faith. I'd spent a fortnight in my attic writing about Shropshire. She said to me: 'I like meeting with you. You lead such an exciting life,' and I smirked when I sensed the desperation in her voice. Jennifer is a woman who wants to be reached and I suddenly knew I'd have no better chance of reaching her than by travelling with her on a long journey, so I said:

'I've been thinking. You're right. We should go to the source of the Thames together.'

She went straight to the bar and came back with a bottle of champagne and said: 'Shelley did the same sort of journey in the summer of 1815, you know?'

Then she kissed me and I felt that this would be the trip I'd always wanted to make. It wasn't until the end of the evening as we parted that she said: 'Before we go, promise me one thing.'

'What's that?'

'You won't bring that horrible little dog of yours along, will you?'

3. Listen, I'll Have to Meet You in Hampton Later

Boogie isn't my dog. Boogie isn't anyone's dog. Boogie is a freelance.

He was found abandoned as a puppy, and taken home to a darkened room in south London and fed crisps. There he grew up the hard way, a London mongrel, devious and streetwise with a strong sense of survival and little in common with other dogs. He would never fetch sticks, only hubcaps.

He came to stay with me in north London a while ago for a weekend and never left. I still don't know how long he's here for. We live our own lives, Boogie and me. For this reason I never thought leaving him behind while Jennifer and I went on our trip would be a problem. To be honest I assumed he'd make his own arrangements.

Besides, my attention during that pre-departure period was directed in other areas, mostly in the search for a boat. I had quickly decided there was only one sort that would suit an expedition to the source of the Thames, and it wasn't an eight-berth fibreglass tub with a chemical toilet and bedside lights and magazine racks in the saloon. I wanted something classical, and I wanted something beautiful. I wanted a camping skiff, and nothing else would do.

Skiffs are low wooden boats based on the design of the traditional passenger craft of the Thames, the wherry. They first appeared on the river in the mid nineteenth century when messing about in boats became a popular pastime and a more stable and forgiving hire-craft was needed. With a canvas top they were easily converted into campers; the upper Thames was there for the exploring and no boat represented the heyday of the river better. In these days of fibreglass, however, skiffs have become an endangered species and I'd all but given up hope of finding one until I came across Mark Edwards, a man who restored old models at his Hampton boatyard. I phoned him and explained that I was planning a trip to the source of the Thames, that I wanted a traditional camping skiff and that I understood he was my man and he said: 'You're lucky you caught me, I was just off down the pub.'

I asked him if he had a boat that would suit and he said: '*Maegan*. *Maegan* is the perfect skiff for what you have in mind.'

'What's so special about *Maegan*?'

'She's a hundred years old.'

'So?'

'So whenever people sitting in their gardens by the riverside see you, they all go: "Look at that boat!" Then they ask you in for champagne.'

Maegan sounded ideal. She slept 'eight at a squeeze, two comfortably', and came fully equipped right down to tupperware. It was only when I explained I wanted to start the trip from Tower Bridge that complications arose. Mark said he could arrange for *Maegan* to be taken down, but then he pointed out that for the inexperienced waterman the tidal river up as far as the first lock in Teddington could prove to be tricky. It was prone to sudden tidal surges and unpredictable currents. It was a commercial as well as a pleasure craft's waterway and we could well find ourselves rowing alongside battleships. We'd need to know what we were doing.

So for the next week I spent a lot of time round at Jennifer's flat studying tide timetables. And there is nothing like tide timetables for dampening one's enthusiasm. Jennifer yawned and asked how long the trip would take and I said that that would depend on where the source was, but I imagined in the region of three weeks. Since Gloucestershire is only eighty miles away this astounded her and she suggested we take a speedboat and do it in an afternoon. I explained to her about locks and other delays, including the four-miles-an-hour speed limit on the river, and she explained to me about the ten thousand pounds in salary she would lose by being away from work for three weeks. At this remark I protested and said that it didn't appear to me she was entering into the spirit of the expedition. I told her that three weeks was hardly a long time in which to unravel a geographical riddle and that, to be honest, I was surprised she hadn't resigned from her job as a gesture of her commitment. Then the phone went and she had to go back to the office.

I persevered though, and each evening stayed up late reading information from the Port of London Authority, reading reports from river pilots and studying navigation manuals. I learnt that a blue and white flag means scuba divers are in the vicinity. I learnt that a bale of hay hanging from beneath a bridge means Men At Work above. I learnt that boats give way to other boats on their starboard bow. I learnt all sorts of codes and practices, and I learnt a variety of regulations and rules. Then one night Jennifer said she'd learnt that a pleasure boat with a sun-deck and a cafeteria selling teas, coffees, alcoholic drinks and an assortment of light refreshments chugged up from Tower Bridge to near Mark Edwards' boatyard in Hampton twice daily and cost just five pounds, and I had to admit that seemed a far more sensible idea.

That was two days before departure and Boogie was still without accommodation. I'd hoped the people at the Kohinoor Curry House might take him in since he spends most of his evenings round their dustbins. Or I thought the local Radio Rentals might put him up since he spends his days sitting outside their window watching the racing. Or perhaps the local police station since he frequently ends up in their cells. But everyone made impressively imaginative excuses, and so I turned first to the telephone and then finally to providence.

Crouch End in north London is a fine place to start a journey. It's on high ground, and as you walk out of your door you feel that wherever you're heading it's going to be downhill. A millennium or two ago, from the top of Crouch Hill you would have been able to look down over a forested valley to where the rivers Fleet and Tyburn joined the Thames and the Roman city of Londinium stood within its defensive walls. On the banks of such a strategically well-placed and piercing river the city flourished. It grew and then spread and ultimately sprawled, and now from the top of Crouch Hill you can see no further than the block of flats across the road.

I took a train to Tower Hill and sat there nervously, reading the adverts, rehearsing how I should break the news about Boogie to Jennifer: 'I didn't want him to come but what would you have done, let him starve? . . .' No, that wouldn't work, she'd say: 'Yes.' She's hard Jennifer is; fair but hard. 'Dogs are for life, you know? When you go away you can't just switch them off and take the plug out . . .' No, that was sarcastic. Jennifer has a strange sense of humour. 'I think you're being unfair to Boogie. You've just never taken the chance to get to know him.'

Maybe that was the way to handle it, be constructive. Boogie was a seasoned traveller after all. A river journey would be a good way for Jennifer and him to get to know each other. It would be a good way for us all to get to know each other.

It's not as if Boogie is a dependent sort of animal. I watched him as he sidled up the carriage to a man with a briefcase on his lap. Boogie put his head on the man's knee and looked him straight in the eye and within two stops the man had opened his case, taken out his packed lunch and fed it to Boogie piece by piece. Some people say it's wrong to let a dog beg. Maybe. The point is, begging has nothing to do with Boogie's performance – it isn't part of his repertoire and he wouldn't humiliate himself so. Middle age may have slowed Boogie down, in so far as he prefers to stay indoors now and watch a good documentary rather than go out and chase a cat, but it has also brought him experience and the realization that the best method of persuasion is not plaintive pleading but hypnotism.

The man with the briefcase didn't make the decision to give Boogie his lunch; he simply had no say in the matter. One look into Boogie's yellow, gas-filled eyes and he was in a trance. From him Boogie moved up the train as passengers rummaged through their pockets in an effort to find something to feed him. I sat back and watched the show. Seeing him perform like this I get the feeling Boogie is never more at home than he is on the London Underground system. It's his natural habitat. I quite expect to get off a train one day and find him busking. His only problem is escalators where he has to be carried. If ever you see a dog at the bottom of an escalator hitch-hiking, pick him up, it's Boogie.

I was at Tower Pier at eleven o'clock on the dot. Half an hour later there was still no sign of Jennifer. I strolled up the pier and watched the river roll: a fat, grey slob of a river with the tide slipping out, leaving a mark on the embankments like a ring around a bath. I followed a wave downstream and sensed an irresistible force. Any notion I had of this journey being an easy ride was forgotten here. I suddenly had the feeling this was going to be a far more demanding project than I'd imagined. My research had shown me that as far as Lechlade we could rely on a well-regulated waterway serviced by the Thames Water Authority, but from there on to Cricklade and beyond there were rumours of an untamed stripling river, and I knew that our chances of success would depend greatly on conditions. I looked in the water and tried to imagine the source in a field, and how somewhere among that flow was a drop that had come all the way from Gloucestershire.

With fifteen minutes to departure there was still no sign of Jennifer. The waterbus to Hampton sat looking bored, framed by the grey and blue twin towers of Tower Bridge. This was the last crossing before the sea, the grandest most famous bridge over the river, and it annoyed me the way it reminded me of a giant cruet. I sat down and counted the pigeons. With five minutes to go I went to telephone. I tried Jennifer's home, her health club and her car phone. Eventually I traced her to her office. Her personal assistant answered.

'Is Jennifer Conway there?' I said.

'Can I ask who's calling?'

'Mark Wallington.'

'Can I ask what company?'

'It's a personal call.'

'Can I ask what it's about?'

'No.'

'Jennifer Conway is engaged, can you call back tomorrow?'

'She was supposed to meet me at Tower Pier an hour ago.'

'It's not in her diary.'

'I want to speak to her.'

'She's just left the room. She'll be back on Friday.'

'Tell her I've smashed into her TVR. I've caused an estimated five thousand pounds' worth of damage, and I thought I'd give her my name and address. But if she's not there . . .'

Muzak came down the line, something from *West Side Story*. On the river a tug ploughed upstream and black-headed gulls circled overhead.

Jennifer came on the line. I said: 'Jennifer, what are you doing at work!?' and Boogie started barking as he always does when he hears her name.

Jennifer said: 'I'm sorry. I had to come in here on the way. Panic stations, I'm afraid. I'll be late. I'll have to meet you later in Hampton. What's that barking?'

'What barking?'

'That barking I can hear.'

'I don't hear any barking.'

'It's familiar barking.'

'It's the foghorn on the boat. It's leaving. I'll see you in Hampton.'

I ran on board and felt the turbulence push us away from the wharf. Boogie sat down next to me with an ice cream in his mouth. On the pier stood a confused eleven-year-old schoolboy. The kid didn't stand a chance.

John Hanning Speke and Richard Burton are the two names that most readily come to mind when one thinks of journeys to the sources of great rivers. I thought of these two great rivals as I headed upstream under London Bridge, how they departed from Zanzibar in 1856 and ventured into regions of Africa no white man had seen

before, how they endured a year or more of privation in
their obsessional quest for the source of the Nile, and how
my journey had nothing whatsoever in common with
theirs.

But I was beginning to relax now. In some ways I felt
pleased to have this time to myself before Jennifer arrived.
I'd felt tense. Now I sat back and watched the sun sparkle
on the water. Boogie too decided to collect himself. He
lay sprawled across the deck in typical fashion – i.e. in
such a position as to cause the maximum inconvenience
to everyone else on the boat. It's a rare gift he has. If you
took him to a field he'd lie down so that he blocked the
gate. Everyone took great pains to step over him and
say: 'Aww', and feed him biscuits which of course just
encouraged him.

A voice came over on the Tannoy: 'Hello, my name's
Ken, any questions don't be frightened to ask. I know
London better than the pigeons. I used to be a cab driver.'
We passed Cleopatra's Needle and Ken said: 'Something
to do with Egypt that is. Word of advice if you're driving
along the Embankment here – you can't turn right at the
lights going up to Charing Cross. I had a nasty accident
there once. Blocked both lanes of traffic for three hours.
Oxyacetylene job. Got a fine for that one.'

Most of the passengers were American and Spanish
tourists. They listened to the commentary and looked at
the view for a while but were far more interested in the
Chelsea Pensioner on board. They kept buying him
drinks. They lit his cigarettes and posed for pictures with
him. He had the same sort of potential for attention as
Boogie. People wanted to stroke him. An American
woman said: 'Well, well, look at that coat, what do you
wear underneath it?'

'I'm eighty-eight I am,' said the Chelsea Pensioner.

'Are you?'

'Course I am. I just said I was.'

We slipped under Westminster Bridge. A barge gave a blast on its siren and Ken took evasive action just in time. He said: 'Here's a building you'll all recognize: the Houses of Parliament. Particularly unpleasant roundabout behind there. I had three accidents in one afternoon there once. Got an endorsement.'

'Eighty-eight! Is that right?' said a Spanish woman to the Chelsea Pensioner.

'Eighty-eight, and I've only had one hip replacement.'

'I'm going to buy you a drink,' she said.

'Suit yourself,' he mumbled and took out his tobacco tin.

With the water so low and the Embankment so high we felt dwarfed by the city. We passed the Battersea Dogs' Home and Boogie hid under the seat. We passed Battersea Power Station and the Chelsea Pensioner said: 'I live there.'

Everyone took a step back.

'Not there, there!' he said, and pointed to Wren's Royal Hospital on the opposite bank. 'It's nice there; too many old people, though.' Someone handed him a can of lager and he said: 'It's not everyone can become a Chelsea Pensioner, you know. You have to have served your King and country for a kick-off. And have a clean record, military and otherwise. They wouldn't let you in if, say, you had a conviction for armed robbery. Forging bank notes would be right out as well. A parking fine and you might be okay, but arson and you wouldn't stand a chance. Treason and they'd show you the door immediately. Littering or not paying your television licence on time you might get away with.'

'Putney Bridge,' said Ken and a raspberry-flavoured Slush Puppy sailed over the parapet and landed on the boat's roof in an explosion of red ice. 'Of particular personal interest to me Putney Bridge is. It's the only bridge in London I've not had an accident on.'

The Chelsea Pensioner escaped from his fans and sat next to me. His coat had a few medals on it and lots of stains. His shoes were highly polished but his collar and cuffs were frayed. He leant over to pat Boogie.

'What sort is he?'

'Italian terrier.'

Actually, Boogie isn't an Italian terrier. In fact he's nothing like a terrier. He's nothing like a dalmatian either, or a beagle or a pekinese or a spaniel. He bears no resemblance whatsoever to a dachshund, and red setters and Boogie have nothing in common whatsoever. He couldn't be more unlike a Pyrenean mountain dog. No one could ever mistake him for a labrador and if you suggested he was descended from a husky you'd make yourself look foolish. The idea of confusing him with a bulldog is absurd and those who propose he has alsatian in him are talking nonsense. You could call him a mongrel but you'd be pushing your luck. Boogie is a dog – just.

'Italian terrier, eh?' said the Chelsea Pensioner.

At this point most people who try to guess Boogie's lineage realize the complexities of the family tree they are faced with, say: 'Thought so', and then try to change the subject.

'Thought so,' said the Chelsea Pensioner. 'I had a cat once,' and he puffed on his roll-up.

I said to him: 'I bet you've seen some changes in your time?' and he nodded and said: 'Everyone asks me that.'

We passed through Barnes and Chiswick and the river was now a place where people lived. Syon Park looked like a rain forest surrounded by property development. At Kew a number of people disembarked, and even more at Richmond where the Star and Garter Home stood high on the hill like a palace and the meadows below were full of buttercups. We passed islands and undergrowth and suddenly the city was gone. The Chelsea Pensioner said: 'By boat is the best way to see London, it's just that when the tide's out all you see is slime.' And then in the afternoon sunshine he nodded off, only waking once when we passed a strange collection of timber and plastic sheeting tied together on a raft and moored under a willow to make a sort of houseboat. A dirty little face poked through. A child waved, smiled and stuck its tongue out. 'Gypsies,' said the Pensioner, 'nothing wrong with gypsies.' He waved back and stuck his own tongue out and then fell asleep again.

It took us five hours to reach Hampton. 'Which may seem like a long time,' said Ken, 'but driving it can take two hours if the South Circular is chocker. Ah! Hampton Court, I know a lot about Hampton Court, or I should do – I hit it once. Got banned for that one.'

I walked down the towpath to Mark Edward's boatyard. It was early evening now and the river was on fire with reflections. Oarsmen and canoeists cut waves that lapped briefly at the bank but the river quickly reclaimed its inertia. Swan feathers floated on the water and there was a smell of diesel and old wood. There was no sign of Jennifer though.

I lugged my stuff into the boatyard and found Mark Edwards covered in wood shavings and smelling of preservative. He looked like the sort who, no matter when you called, would be covered in wood shavings and smelling of preservative. He smiled and said proudly: 'I'll show you *Maegan*.'

He led me down to where the skiffs were moored, and pointed to twenty-two feet of sparkling mahogany with the name *Maegan* inscribed in uncial on the backboard. She was broad-hipped and round-shouldered and looked

more like a piece of furniture than a boat. She was exquisite. Mark said: 'Have you had a good look?'

'Not really . . .'

'Right, let's go to the pub.'

I pinned a note for Jennifer on the door and we went
to a pub in Hampton village. The landlord said: 'it's
always quiet on a Thursday.'

Boogie went round the pub and despite there being
only three people in he managed to score a crab sandwich,
a piece of quiche and some pâté and pickle. I asked Mark
if he had any tips for me and he said: 'When you get to
Pangbourne call in at the Swan, best pub on the Thames.
And when you go past Vince Hill's house in Bray, wave,
'cos likely as not he'll wave back from his veranda.' I
suggested he might have information of a more technical
nature, perhaps pertaining to the stretch of river above
Lechlade. 'Oh,' he said and leant over his glass: 'It's been
a dry spring, lack of water is going to be your problem.'
Then with the aid of two beer mats and some dry-roasted
peanuts he demonstrated how I could build a makeshift
flash-lock – an age-old locking system for hauling craft
up river.

'That's the theory anyway,' he said, 'but it's a tricky
trip to Cricklade.'

'How tricky?'

'Well, put it like this. I've never known anyone make
it. Just you and the dog, is it?'

'No, a girlfriend's coming with me.'

'Sort of like *Three Men in a Boat*.'

'Well, sort of, except there are only two of us and one
is a woman.'

'It's the centenary of *Three Men in a Boat*, you know?
What you should do is dress up in a striped blazer and
put on a boater and grow a Victorian moustache and re-
create the trip. A number of people use my boats to do

that. One a week this year. Bunch of prats if you ask me. Here, your glass is empty. We can't have that. Mine's a pint of Websters. Ta.'

Three Men in a Boat was the book synonymous with the Thames, and many people had made references to it when Jennifer and I had announced our intentions. I'd not been aware it was the centenary of Jerome's trip but now knowing only made me feel more uncomfortable. A re-creation was the last thing I wanted to do. I loved his story and to re-create it would be like seeing the film after reading the book and I knew I'd be disappointed.

I went back with the drinks and Mark said: 'But *Maegan*'s a good boat. My oldest. If anyone can get you there she can. She deserves a trip like this. I found her under a pile of rot in a Godalming boatyard. She had moss on her gunwales. Abandoned she'd been. She still bears the scars.'

I said: 'A bit like Boogie.'

He studied Boogie. 'Yes, I can imagine him with moss on his gunwales.' Boogie put his head on Mark's lap and Mark gave him his crisps.

'He likes you,' I said. 'You wouldn't like to look after him for three weeks, would you?'

'You take him with you. He'll be good company when your girlfriend leaves you.'

'What do you mean?'

'A camping skiff holiday can destroy any relationship. I never told you about Doreen and me did I? . . . Well, look at that, there's a dog hair in my beer.'

We were interrupted as a powerful motorbike pulled up outside, and the peace of the pub was broken as the door swung open and there stood a large leather-clad figure. He strode over to us. In one hand he had a crash helmet, in the other, a carrier bag. He looked at me through his moustache. 'Mark Wallington?'

'Yes.'

He handed me the bag. Inside was a pile of spare ribs, some barbecue sauce, some coleslaw, a baked potato, some strawberry cheesecake and a poem – 'Cars head down the rubble roads, travellers to far-off places. The darkness hides their dreams, their windscreens hide their faces, – Bon Appetit. Call me. Love from Jennifer.'

'That's a dreadful poem,' said Mark, leaning over my shoulder.

'It is, isn't it?' said the biker. 'It shows an inability to properly express herself at a time when she most wants to. If you ask me she's under stress and needs support.'

'Who are you?'

'I'm Michael, the courier for her firm. But most people say I'm too intuitive. Sign here please.'

Michael roared off and we walked back to the boatyard in the failing light. Mark showed me how to turn the skiff into a camper. What looked like an extremely complicated manoeuvre turned out to be very simple, involving a set of hoops inserted at intervals along the length of the boat to form a frame, and a canvas cover pulled over the lot. *Maegan* looked like a fairground caterpillar when all was finished.

Mark said: 'You'll be getting an early start I suppose, so I won't see you in the morning. Good luck. Make sure *Maegan* gets there. She can take anything you can give her. She's based on the design of the Viking longship, you know? See that curve on the gunwale? That's where you'd hang your axe if you were a pillaging Norseman.' He turned to go and then stopped and said: 'One more piece of advice. Watch out for your spoons – they go missing on trips of this nature.'

'Spoons?'

'Spoons.' As he spoke there were two sploshes. One was the sound of a dessert spoon falling in the river. The other was the sound of a three-stone mongrel doing just the same. I spun round and through the watery muck a little black head appeared in panic. I hauled him out and shouted to Mark: 'Run!'

'What!'

'Run!' But it was too late, and a gallon of turbid river water was sprayed over him and the rest of his boatyard as Boogie shook himself dry.

'Forget what I said about him being good company,' said Mark. 'He's going to be a bloody nuisance.' And he walked off home.

I sat on the river bank and had my spare ribs and made a mess of myself. Then later I found a phone box and tried to call Jennifer. I tried her home, her office and her health club, and finally reached her on her car phone. She was in Birmingham.

'Jennifer! What's happened?' I said, and Boogie started to bark.

Jennifer said: 'Listen. I'm sorry. Something big has come up. I can't make it tonight. You'll have to leave without me. I'll meet you at the weekend. I'm really sorry. I wish I was with you. Did you get the spare ribs? What did you think of the poem? I wrote it in a hurry. It's not finished. What's that barking?'

'Nothing.'

'I'm sure I heard barking.'

'The boatyard guard dog. I'll call you tomorrow.'

I took Boogie for a walk along the towpath.

'I suppose you think I'm wasting my time with her?'

Boogie went down to the bank and gargled with some river water.

'I suppose you think she's using me.'

Boogie shoved his nose into a rubbish bin and brought out an old running shoe which he started to chew.

'Well you're wrong; you just don't understand her.

She's got integrity, Jennifer has. And you'd be well advised to try to get on with her. She's good company.'

Boogie licked something off the path and started to foam at the mouth.

'Better company than you anyway.'

We strolled back to the boat. I lit the lamp and the shadows leapt across the water. A moth crashed into the glass and plunged into the bilges. A swan drifted past like a cloud. Somewhere a bicycle bell rang and an owl made a noise nothing like a hoot.

I looked round for Boogie and saw him watching from the bank, nonplussed. Then he saw me unpack my stuff and climb under the canvas and he started to chuckle. Oh how he chuckled. He grasped his sides and he began to roar. He held his stomach, lay down on the grass and rolled and giggled. He stood up, regained his composure then pointed at the boat and burst into a fit of hysterics.

Then I told him to get in.

I found him an hour later in the waiting room of Hampton station.

4. Be on Windsor Bridge at Seven – Prompt

The Thames is 216 miles long, an unimpressive length for a waterway of such stature. Diminutive, for instance, when compared to the Amazon. Insignificant when spoken of in the same breath as the Yangtze. A joke when placed side by side with the Mississippi. Nothing but a pathetic brook by the standards of the Zambezi.

The Thames is an undramatic river as well. In its meander to the sea it travels through water meadows for much of its length, falling only 350 feet from top to bottom. In that time it slips unmysteriously through places like Staines, Slough, Reading and Pangbourne, passing no waterfalls, no lakes and no swamps. The classic Thames animal is the duck. The classic plant, the geranium. The only tribe, the commuter. The Thames is a place where anything other than serenity is considered embarrassing. During my research it didn't take long to realize that to follow this river to its source had all the potential of one of the dullest journeys ever made.

And yet no river has influenced world history as much as the Thames, except for perhaps the Euphrates and the Rhine, and perhaps the Tiber, and then of course there's the Nile, and you can't rule out the Ganges. The reason for this is that the Thames refuses to compromise. It is a

celebration of understatement. Its qualities are subtle in
the extreme. In books about the Thames you rarely come
across the adjectives awesome, stunning or spectacular.
Peaceful you see quite often, and tranquil frequently,
evocative is a favourite and ethereal crops up now and
again, but breathtaking – never.

So I planned a departure from Hampton in keeping
with the ambience of the river. I planned to rise at first
light and get under way while the sun was a red button
on the horizon and the mist still crawled on the water. I
wanted to be the only boat on the river. I wanted to see
the Thames without its wrinkles, without the sound of
traffic. I wanted to be on it before the ducks even.

Instead I overslept, sleeping long after people who are
about to set off to the source of a great river are supposed
to sleep. This wasn't entirely my fault though, *Maegan*
quickly established herself as a cosy and curvacious craft
built for comfort not speed, and with the canvas overcoat
stretched on top of her she cocooned all within in a tunnel
of watertight sleep, so that it was still the dead of night
inside the tent while on the outside buses were rolling
past on the main road and newspapers were being rammed
through letter boxes.

When I finally had the sense to lift up the tent flap
and inspect the situation for myself, a laser-like beam of
sunshine burst in and I was confronted with one of those
yellow, green and blue days so perfect you feel envious
of nature and the ease with which she can conjure up such
beauty, and this makes you depressed and you want to
go back to bed again.

I squinted at the reflections on the water. The river was
still motionless; the same scum of wood chips and swan
feathers surrounded the boat. In the workshop I could
hear people building boats. I hurriedly dismantled the tent
and dumped it in a bundle in the stern and arranged myself

for departure. But I wasn't quick enough. A lad from the workshop came out with a cup of tea and said: 'Still here then?'

'Yes.'

'Huh.'

'Huh.'

'I bet you Robin Knox-Johnston never had a lie-in the morning he left Plymouth to become the first man to sail single-handed round the globe.'

'No I don't expect he did.'

Rowing – or rather sculling – isn't a particularly complicated activity, not on paper anyway. It's largely a question of rhythm, of getting both oars – or rather sculls – to do the same manoeuvre at the same time, then compensating for one's superior strength in one arm with an extra half stroke every five with the inferior arm, not forgetting to navigate a course in one direction while looking in the other, plus, in my case, coping with a hydrophobic dog trying his utmost to get out of the boat while at the same time trying his utmost to stay in it.

The result, that first morning, as I covered the stretch from Hampton through Sunbury and headed on to Weybridge, was a highly uncoordinated one. The onlooker on the bank would have seen a boat heading in the general direction of Gloucestershire but doing it the hard way, staggering from one side of the river to the other, ricocheting off islands and turning the occasional circle.

Fortunately there was little traffic about and, although my technique meant I was seeing rather more of places like the Molesey Reservoirs than I intended, it mattered little since the great thing about going to the source of a river is that it is very difficult to lose your bearings. As long as the channel gets progressively thinner and more shallow the traveller can assume that he or she is on course. I calculated that all I had to do was keep heading uphill and at any confluence follow the largest piece of water, and sooner or later I would reach the inevitable pool in a field.

Besides I was in no hurry. I had a couple of days to familiarize myself with the river: to harden my hands, to become au fait with the terms and techniques of the activity, to victual the boat and learn how to manage life afloat. That way all would be in order by the time Jennifer arrived, and I could impress her with my waterman's appeal. Boogie, too, would have time to acclimatize. The truth is he's not really used to the outdoors. Scenic places confuse him. He needed a little time to find his river legs, and then scenes such as the one at the first lock we entered would less likely be repeated.

This was Sunbury lock, and I arrived in a fashion befitting *Meagan's* Viking heritage – full pelt, bow first, straight into the doors. A jolly little man wearing a cap and a shirt with epaulettes peered over the walls: 'Sorry, I was putting in my bedding plants,' he said and proceeded to operate the hydraulic gates. I paddled *Maegan* into the lock. The gates swung shut, there was a tremor beneath us and slowly we rose.

'What sort of dog's that?' said the lock-keeper.

'Argentinian ridgeback.'

'Thought it might be,' he said, then changed the subject: 'Going upstream?' I told him I was going to the source and asked him if he had any advice to offer. He contemplated this for a while then said: 'Yes, make sure you call in at the Swan in Staines, best pub on the river.'

He opened the upstream gates and that was when I noticed Boogie had jumped from the boat and was standing on the bank. 'Stay!' I said with authority and he immediately made a return leap. This time he didn't make it though, or rather half of him didn't. He remained suspended above the lock in a splits, two legs on land two on the boat, his attempts to reunite both sets pushing the boat further away.

I've never seen an animal's body elongate with such style. Boogie's back legs stretched until he was holding on to the bank with his claws. His front set did likewise, and when they failed him and he was falling towards the water, his teeth grabbed hold of *Maegan's* hundred-year-old mahogany. He resembled a canine gangplank for a while but ultimately he ended up where he was getting used to ending up. And if I'd thought the slick round Mark Edwards' boatyard was gruesome, it was spa water compared to the version found in locks. When Boogie surfaced and crawled up the steps to the lock-keeper's garden he looked like the Creature from the Black Lagoon, only less attractive. The lock-keeper took one look at him and dropped his trowel in fright.

'Run!' I shouted to the lock-keeper and ducked down in the boat, but it was too late and he and his house and half of Sunbury took a filthy shower.

At Shepperton I parked – or rather moored – on a rare piece of public bank among all the river frontages and No Mooring Strictly Private Stop Here And You're Asking For Trouble signs. I put the kettle on and lay back in the boat, the air so still, the water so calm that every noise was amplified: a man took his dustbins out in a house behind the trees; an expensive car door slammed beyond the next hedge; a hammer hit a piece of metal in an engineering works somewhere upstream and the noise carried over the river like birdsong. Above me jets from all nations circled looking for a parking space, or climbed and banked and quickly became a speck in the blue. At a lower altitude insects revved their motors, and on the water ducks flew in like seaplanes. It was a perfect spring day in suburbia; the ideal habitat for beasts such as *Midnight Rider II*.

At first all I was aware of was the growl of a powerful engine held on a leash. Then I was hit by a vast shadow and every creature in the vicinity dived for cover. A series of waves slapped against *Maegan* and leapt over her side and she bucked and smacked against the bank. The kettle fell off the stove, my hat fell in the water and I looked up to see a shining glass and plastic construction covered in antennae. It was the size of a cross-Channel car ferry and travelled through the water with its chin in the air. Along the bow was written the name *Midnight Rider II*.

I'd heard about these boats – the brochures called them cruisers, their critics called them Gin Palaces, a builder would have called them maisonettes. I'd imagined them to be as splendid as this, but never as sinister. *Midnight Rider II* was taller than she was long. She was fitted with radar and with lifeboats and everything attached to her sparkled to the extent that she dazzled oncoming traffic. On the deck in the conning tower were a woman in a swimsuit, and a man with mirror sunglasses. The boat was presumably on automatic pilot for no one was at the wheel, but then I couldn't see a wheel, just these two walking around the deck holding coils of rope and bumping into each other. They looked at me and waved and I sort of waved back and that was my mistake. *Midnight Rider II* slipped round the bend of the river and out of sight among the trees, but minutes later she returned and after much manoeuvring and general destruction of the environment and me – but mostly me – she moored next to me – but mostly on top of me.

'Sorry,' said the captain. 'Didn't disturb you did we? I wasn't too sure if this was public at first, but since you were here, well . . .'

From the saloon I could hear the television on.

'Funny-looking boat you've got there,' he went on. 'It's . . . it's not got a motor, has it?'

'It's a camping skiff. It's a hundred years old. It's got oars – I mean sculls.'

'Hmm,' he said. 'Mine was built in 1986. It's got all sorts of things. It's got a fire extinguisher for instance. Reception is lousy on the telly though. Where are you going?'

'The source.'

'Which way's that?'

I pointed towards Slough.

'I never go very far upstream. We live in Walton. We just got this to potter about in. TV reception gets bad upstream. The Crystal Palace signal gets weak round the Cotswolds, see. We had a booster put up in our area to reconvert the frequency. You need a different aerial but it's worth it.'

A funny-looking bird swam up to us. It was orange and white and smaller than a duck. It had the worst haircut of any bird I'd ever seen.

'I've seen a few of those over the years. You know what they are?' said the captain of *Midnight Rider II*.

'No,' I said.

'Neither do I. It's not a swan, that's for sure.'

'No, it's not a swan.'

'No.'

We looked at the bird for a while. There were probably no two less well-versed watermen on the river that morning. I dug out my bird book and identified the creature as a great crested grebe.

'It's a great crested grebe,' I said.

'Mmm.'

'With its legs situated under its tail the great crested grebe is ungainly and rarely seen on land, but supreme under water,' I read.

'Is it?'

'Its nest is usually a floating raft of vegetation. Both sexes incubate the eggs.'

'Mmm.'

A little black bird with a patch on its head appeared on the scene. I identified it as a coot or a moorhen. When the grebe saw it, it thumped its head in.

'That was unpleasant,' said the captain of *Midnight Rider II*. Then he looked at his watch and called out to his wife: 'Are those Yorkshires ready yet? The film's nearly started.'

She came to the hatch and said: 'Alan, come here a minute. There's a strange dog in our saloon watching television.'

I rowed – or rather sculled – on to Weybridge, a neat, smart, newly painted, traffic-light-controlled, streets-cleaned-every-night, bins-emptied-every-Thursday town with a W. H. Smith's, a Boots, a Peter Dominic and a Benetton.

This was my first riverside town and I was interested to see if, despite its suburban dormitory status, Weybridge had retained its former spirit as a commercial port. I walked up the high street looking for the one building where all travellers new to a town can go to hear the local news and meet the local folk – the supermarket.

I swung a trolley round the aisles, loaded it with provisions, then joined checkout two and stood amongst sun-tanned mothers with their teenage daughters. I was hemmed in by talk of time-share apartments and contraception.

We shuffled forward. Muzak from *Doctor Zhivago* filled every empty space. The man in front of me sneezed and his wife said: 'Did you know that the strongest sneeze ever recorded was over a hundred miles an hour and had the power of a force-seven gale?' At the front of the queue a customer was paying by cheque, the next paid by Access and the next by customer credit, for which forms were filled out in triplicate. The next customer had a price query, and the next was a friend of the checkout girl, Lorraine, and they chatted about their friend Dave who smashed up his dad's Ford Granada on Tuesday. I was just getting the impression that Weybridge folk were a civil and patient lot, with a rustic quality belying their proximity to London, when suddenly the two nicely dressed women behind me cracked and a battle for position began. 'I was here before you, you bitch!' 'Don't call me a bitch, you slut!' Mr Davis the manager went straight in and put up the Till Closed sign. We all scrummed down and I joined checkout four. With two people to go before me the till ran out of change and checkout girl Rachael sat there with her arms folded looking out of the window thinking of Mike, the lad with the long arms from dairy produce. The woman behind me who only had a tin of tuna fish and a sliced loaf in her basket said: 'You wouldn't mind if I go in front of you, would you? I've only got two items,' but I didn't even bother to turn round. I wasn't going to be taken advantage of just because I was new in town. Besides, Mr Davis had come over with a bag of change and there was just an elderly man in front of me. But Rachael was giving him a rough ride; 'You haven't weighed your tomatoes have you?' she barked at him.

'What?'

'You haven't weighed your tomatoes!'

'What?'

'Go and weigh them!' And she threw the things at him and sent him off. I moved into his space and smiled at her and she snarled back and walked off for a tea break. Julie took her place. She counted out her money, changed the cash-roll and was about to pull the first item out of my basket when she put her head in her hands and burst into tears. Everyone at checkout four just stood there looking at her. None of us had any idea how to comfort a supermarket checkout person. I think someone might have said: 'There there!' but then one of us spotted checkout three was open and we all scrummed down again. Mr Davis moved in and led Julie away. 'I understand,' he was saying. 'But it's like riding a horse. You've got to get right back in the saddle.'

I had entered the supermarket a cool individual with the swagger of a man about to journey to the source of a great river. I walked back to the boat a seething, sweating wreck with an in-depth knowledge of life in Weybridge and a desire to kick innocent animals. Boogie, fortunately, is very understanding in situations like this. When he sees me in this state he gives me his 'it's all right; I know what you're going through' look. 'You're all pent up and you want to kick me, don't you? Well you go right ahead if it makes you feel better. You relieve your stress on my kidneys, that's what I'm here for. Go ahead, kick the dog, I enjoy it really.' And I feel suddenly full of remorse and think about people in the world less fortunate than myself, and I bend down and stroke him and pat him on the head and end up giving him a packet of biscuits.

We sculled through the afternoon. A policeman in a patrol boat gave a 'good for you' wave. A work party on a British Waterways Board launch whistled at me and held up their cups of tea in an 'all the best' gesture. A man sitting on his lawn in front of a bungalow by a sign that said 'private' in italics, waved at me and probably considered inviting me in for a glass of champagne but then thought better of it.

My real friends though were the lock-keepers, and it was clear after only a day on the river that they were all friendly, helpful and good-humoured, and didn't mind me smashing into their gates. They'd just nod knowingly and admire *Maegan*, and when I asked them if they thought I'd get as far upstream as Cricklade, some would say: 'Never! You'll get dragged down by weed and the boat will break her back on the rocks and your oars will snap in the narrows and the local farmers will shoot you; you'd be a fool to even think about it.' While others would say: 'Of course you'll make it, no trouble.' They all lived on islands in the most idyllic cottages and unlike most people in jobs where you get to wear a hat they weren't inclined to make comments like: 'You can't leave that here!' or 'That's what you think!' or 'Don't you understand plain English!?' If they wanted to make you aware of something they did it diplomatically, in just the way the keeper at Shepperton lock did to a blue-haired woman in a little cabin cruiser. She was busy at her stove as her boat rose up the chamber. The lock-keeper bent down and said: 'Just a word of friendly advice, Madam, but I wouldn't use the stove whilst you're in the lock as there can be a build-up of petrol fumes and there's a good chance that you and your little boat will be blown to bits.'

That evening I reached the village of Laleham. Racing sculls whizzed around me like wasps and I suddenly felt tired. I felt as though I'd travelled fifty miles, which is the feeling a beginner gets from having travelled only seven. A grassy bank in front of a riverside house was the ideal spot to moor for the night and I tied up and rolled out the canvas. Immediately a lawnmower of the kind popularized by cricket groundsmen came hurtling towards me. At the controls was a man with a frenzied look. Grass cuttings flew in all directions as he burned a trail in the lawn to my boat.

'Don't even think about mooring there!' he said.

'. . .'

'Can't you read?' And he pointed to a sign stuck in the ground a few yards away on which nothing was written.
'. . .'

'Public mooring stops there.'

On the other side of the signpost the words Public Mooring were indeed written. He wanted me to move *Maegan* six feet downstream, a manoeuvre which owing to my poor technique took fifteen minutes, and involved an inconvenience factor which Boogie and I made the most of with looks of absolute fatigue and despair. By the time I'd re-moored, the man on the lawnmower was ridden with guilt. 'Sorry about all this, old chap,' he said, 'but we can't be too careful, you know? Here, throw me your rope and I'll tie you up. Got water have you? How about dog food? We can let you have a can if you're out. There's a pub in the village by the way. Nice pub – does a good selection of baked potatoes with a variety of fillings, mushroom and sour cream, chilli and cheese, that sort of job. Peaceful sort of village, Laleham. Nothing of earth-shattering importance has ever happened here; it's never appeared on the *Nine O'clock News* or anything. Although there was a near miss between a British Caledonian 737 and a Cessna light aircraft once which would have focused world attention on us had they hit. Anyway . . .'

I went to call Jennifer. I tried her home, her office and her car and found her at her health club. She said: 'Where are you? You sound miles away.'

'I'm in Laleham.'

'Laleham! That's where Matthew Arnold came from! He's buried by the local church. "Life ran gaily as the sparkling Thames." '

'Listen, meet me in Windsor tomorrow evening, on the bridge at seven.'

'I'll be there. I should be back from Paris by then.'

'Paris!'

'Just for the day. It's business.'

'Jennifer! You can't behave like this.'

Boogie started barking at the phone box at this point.

'What's that barking?'

'I've got to go. The churchyard is closing. Be on the bridge tomorrow. I'll tell you all about Matthew Arnold's grave.'

I found the Arnold family plot near the church door. Children ran about between the mounds of earth. I was surrounded by screams and flintstone. The sun was setting and I was amazed. Amazed because I was standing in Laleham, a village I'd never heard of before and would never have had any reason to come to, and yet I was having a moment I knew I'd never forget. I felt giddy.

I went into a pub; it was almost empty. The barman said: 'It's always quiet on a Friday.' I bought some beer and before I'd got the glass to my lips I began to feel giddy again. Then the room began to sway. I bought some potato and mint flavoured crisps and went out into the garden, and the garden was swaying too.

Boogie went walkabout and managed to score a chilli-burger, a piece of garlic bread, some scampi and some cold cuts. A woman with a steak sandwich gave him half, and her man said 'What are you doing? I'd have had that!'

'The dog's got that look about him,' she said.

'You gave a steak sandwich to a dog. I don't believe it! It's not even our dog!'

Then the table began to sway, then Laleham began to sway. I left my drink and returned to the boat and only then when I was back on water did I feel at ease. I diagnosed I had landsickness. The treatment? An evening with Delia Smith.

I sat in the lamplight with Delia Smith's *One is Fun!* cookbook in one hand and a pan full of piquant liver with a sherry sauce in the other. It tasted wonderful. Afterwards I lay in the dark in my sleeping bag as water lapped at *Maegan* and I felt I knew Delia Smith far better than I had before. It's an amazing thing, travel.

Next morning as I sat on the bank trying to untie the impossible knots I'd tied with such ease the night before, the driver of a canary-yellow cruiser called *Hesnotin* came to visit. He stood next to me and said nothing.

'What time is it?' I asked.

'Ten past nine. Breakfast telly has just finished.' He scrunched up his face, sniffed, scratched his stomach and made his eyebrows jump and said: 'That weatherman, that effeminate fella – not that I've anything against effeminate sorts – but anyway, that weatherman with the permed hair, he just said it's going to thunder and lightning. Glad I'm not in a rowing boat. Which way are you going?'

'Upstream.'

'River's moving faster today. Glad I'm not going upstream.'

I climbed back into my boat and set off and my cereal spoon dropped over the side. The river certainly didn't feel faster today, in fact it felt a lot easier. Maybe I was getting the hang of this sculling business. Maybe one day was all I needed to get fit. Maybe I felt like this because I was going the wrong way.

This was a bad mistake. For a brief moment I'd experienced how much easier it was going downstream.

For some folk Staines is the ideal holiday resort. For Boogie – who is content the minute he sees a pedestrian precinct or an NCP to play in, and who likes underpasses and bypasses and flyovers, and has a soft spot for No Entry Except For Access signs – it was the perfect spot. Likewise for a number of humans moored in their shiny launches outside the Swan. Launches were a step down from cruisers. They were all rather featureless, but this was probably because they were all hired from the company that monopolized the market. Some were dinky, others were modelled on the whale, but they were all uniformly painted in blue and white and their names all had the prefix Maid: *Maid Lucilla, Maid Yvonne, Maid Natasha.* They were like watertight caravans and were crewed by very friendly people in thick pullovers who all waved as I sculled past and called out greetings of the 'it's all right for the dog, eh?' and, 'it's a dog's life isn't it?' or 'get the dog to do some work, I should' or 'dog's got the right idea, hasn't he?' variety.

A number were moored by the London Stone, the point where, before the the river was locked, the reach of the tide ended. The date on the stone is 1285, although the real model was removed to a museum a number of years ago to protect it from vandals. A plastic replica now stands in its place, and that too is surrounded by bars. When that's smashed up they'll probably pin up a photograph of the monument and place an armed guard on it. The stone was the one-time marker of the western limit of the City of London on the Thames, an honour which now unofficially belongs to the M25 that crosses the river a few hundred yards upstream. A motorway is harder to vandalize than an historic monument but one lad was having a go at it as I passed. He was under the bridge scrawling some grafitti on the concrete slabs. He saw me coming and shoved his chalk in his pocket.

As we slipped into the shadow of the motorway the concrete rumbled, and the bridge created an echo like a cave. I could hear the drops of water drip from my sculls. The lad nodded at me and looked nervous and said: 'I'm sheltering, I am.'

'It's not raining.'

'That's what you think. Dog's got the right idea, eh? How old is he?'

'Ten.'

'How old is that for a dog?'

'Er . . . ten.'

I was travelling slowly enough to have conversations of this nature. In fact I was travelling ridiculously slowly – a mile an hour was all I was managing. Even taking into account my heading against the current this was disappointing, and when a woman pushing a pram along the towpath overtook me I slumped and said: 'I want to know why you're pushing a pram and you're overtaking me?' And she stopped, shook her head and said: 'Because you're not leaning back, you're not feathering your blades, you're not keeping out of the main current, your knees aren't together and your boat's not balanced, that's why.'

For the rest of the morning I tried to correct these faults, although the last of them I was unable to do anything about, for the balance of the boat was dependent on the items within it remaining still, and one of these items was Boogie. As he grew to trust *Maegan* a little more he experimented, leaning over the side until he caught his reflection in the water. This so frightened him he'd lurch to the other side and the boat would follow. He also did a nice line in running from bow to stern whenever another boat passed with a dog on it, and so for most of the time *Maegan*, despite sitting on a flat calm of a river, was behaving as though caught in her own Bermuda Triangle of agitation.

'Please don't run up and down the boat, Boogie,' I'd say very reasonably, and he'd give me his cute cow-eyed expression which I knew from experience means 'don't tell me what to do, sunbeam!' People often ask me why Boogie is so disobedient. The reason is not, as they imagine, because of his inability to understand commands

– he does that only too well – his contrariness is purely due to his demand to have the right to choose. He doesn't expect to be given orders; he expects simply to be consulted. Take stick-fetching for instance. To Boogie, stick-fetching is the most demeaning form of canine submissiveness and he insists I join him in his campaign to abolish such a mindless practice. At one point that afternoon, as we slipped into Berkshire, we met a woman throwing sticks into the river for her dog. She flung the things out into the middle and the dog sprang into the water and made for the other side, dodging motorboats. Having retrieved the stick, the dog would then return, exhausted, to the woman and drop it at her feet with a 'there, I've fetched it for you, now don't throw it away again' look. At which the woman immediately lobbed it straight back in the water and the dog sighed and gave her his 'all right, but this is definitely the last time' expression, and dived in again.

The woman looked up with a charming smile when we approached and said: 'Does your dog fetch sticks?' and I had to reply: 'No, my dog thinks fetching sticks is degrading to his species. He doesn't enjoy being treated like a circus animal, and before you throw that stick again for your dog he'd like you seriously to consider the implications of your action.'

'He enjoys it,' she said as the dog disappeared under a paddle steamer with a wedding party on board.

This campaign against stick-fetching was the first in a long line of anti-dogist stands that Boogie has made. His reasoning being that dogs shouldn't exist merely to play a role in the lives of human beings. After an initial protest, I have gradually come to understand and fully support him in his political career. People too easily dismiss Boogie as just an ugly little mongrel with a flatulence problem, but he's a sincere animal with a generosity of spirit, and, with regard to his position in the boat, I knew that if I were to put forward a reasonable case as to why he should cease his excursions from one end to the other, he would comply. Runnymede, I decided, would be a good place to address the problem. Runnymede would get him in a good mood. Runnymede, the Meadow of the Runes, the Council-field, the ancient site for the signing of treaties where in 1215 the earliest of constitutional documents, Magna Carta, was signed by the barons of the nation and their King John.

Quite why they had to do this in the middle of a field is not clear, although, the general theory is that the barons so distrusted their King and the King so distrusted his barons that neither party would go round to the other's place for fear of their lives. The occasion seems to have been a miserable affair from start to finish, with the charter itself showing all the bureaucratic flair of a local government report on a proposed leisure centre. It was the sort of document that created freedom by law in one clause, and abolished fishtraps in rivers, in the next.

Its boldest assertion though was to put the King in check by the creation of a parliamentary assembly, and although, initially, freedom was only granted to all as long as they did what they were told, the day it was signed was the day the nation first asserted the principle of constitutional government, which makes it probably the most important treaty ever signed in the history of the world and so it would have been nice if those involved could have been a bit less grim-faced about the whole thing.

Some say that the site of the actual signing is on Magna Carta island in mid-Thames, but I hope that isn't true since it would mean that the spot where civil liberty was created is now out of bounds to the general public. I'd much rather believe the other theory which claims the charter was signed in Runnymede meadows, an expanse of grass and woodland where a man and his dog are free to wander all they like.

It was by the Magna Carta Memorial that I put it to Boogie that on a journey of this nature one has to make sacrifices for the good of the expedition. The point being that running up and down the boat was undermining our chances of reaching the source of the river, whereas, sitting still in one position would in fact be contributory to the effort. The decision was, I stressed, entirely up to him, and if he chose to run up and down the boat creating havoc then he had every right as a dog to do so, but it would generally be more acceptable if he didn't.

In response he conveyed to me the opinion that he liked running up and down the boat creating havoc and couldn't give a toss about the expedition.

That evening I found a place to moor by the quaintly named Black Potts railway bridge from where there was a glorious view across the fields to Windsor. The castle stood thinly wrapped in a sepia shroud by the sunset. As darkness fell the walls were floodlit and I walked into town drawn by the glow.

The night air was sticky with a storm and the town was at boiling point, its bridge so crowded it seemed to sag with the heat and the stress. I waited outside a pub called the Donkey House where tables and chairs lined the riverside and there was a background of foreign languages and fairy-lights. A crowd were sitting on the quayside singing old Beatles numbers as from downstream a disco boat appeared – more lights and more Golden Oldies. It was the same paddle steamer as I'd seen earlier in the day. The wedding party had been put ashore and a few bulbs changed and the boat had quickly assumed a new role.

I was there on the bridge on the dot of seven. By eight

Jennifer hadn't showed. The pubs began to spill over. The castle glowered above as people without shirts leant against Wren's Guildhall clutching pint pots. There was going to be a storm or a fight, you couldn't tell which. It turned out to be a fight as from the George someone flew out on to the street. There were shouts and smashes of glass and a group of youths ran across the bridge.

I turned to get out of their way and bumped straight into a familiar figure in leathers wearing a crash helmet and clutching a carrier bag.

'Mark Wallington, right?'

'Yes.'

'Me again, Michael.' And he handed me the bag. 'She's got problems. She needs you. Remember that before you get angry. I've a feeling she has an unlocked trauma. Sign here, please.'

I signed and he nodded and said: 'I've been through it as well. It's not easy. If you want someone to talk to let me know.' Then he strode off.

Inside the bag was a note that read: ' "Is it so small a thing To have enjoyed the sun, To have liv'd light in the spring, To have lov'd, to have thought, to have done?" Enjoy the Bombay duck. Call me.'

Boogie and I sat on the bench next to a Japanese couple who smiled at us for twenty minutes as we ate crispy duck, plum sauce, pancakes, spring onions and mushrooms. Afterwards I found a phone box outside the castle gate.

Windsor Castle is attractive because each window you look through you can see some sort of life – you feel the laundry room is full of steam and the kitchen full of cooking smells and there's someone on the landing doing the Hoovering. You get the feeling someone really lives there, which is more than you can say about Jennifer's flat. The answering machine came on. 'Hello, this is Jennifer

Conway, I'm not able to take your call but if you'd like to leave a message I'll get back to you. And if that's Mark, I'm sorry but I've been delayed again, can't help it, something big. I'm really sorry. I should make it on Monday. Have an adventure planned for the afternoon. What do you think of the poem? It's not me – it's Matthew Arnold. But then of course you knew that.'

Concorde passed overhead and two large bats flew into the floodlights of the castle. An owl made a noise nothing like a hoot and I walked out of the town into the darkness and followed the towpath back to the boat. 'She's been delayed, that's all – can't be helped. I know you think her intentions are questionable but you're wrong, you'll see.' Boogie licked something horrible off the path and retched.

In the small hours of the night the storm broke. I awoke to a crack of thunder overhead and rain fired on to the canvas like shot. I lay there in a sweat, waiting for the first drop to pierce *Maegan's* skin, but she remained taut as a drum and took the battering without a protest. At one point during the night I lifted up the flap and saw the castle alive with lightning. The railway bridge hissed and steamed and the river swallowed and filled by the minute. At one point a flash illuminated a supermarket trolley poking out from the water like a skeleton. I lay there wondering what possessed people to throw supermarket trolleys into canals and rivers. There must be some strange thrill attached to it. I decided that at some time on this trip I would go to a supermarket and steal a trolley and push it into a secluded stretch of the river and discover the sensation for myself.

Next morning I was up at dawn, a time of the day which doesn't reach anyone sleeping in *Maegan* until eight thirty.

I breathed in a new day, felt the sun on my face. If you could ignore the goods trains rumbling over Black Potts

Bridge, the traffic on the Datchet road, the jet engines overhead and the blue and white bathtub that roared by crewed by Chelsea supporters chasing the ducks, it was a peaceful Sunday scene.

I sat in the boat during the morning and tried to make notes, but I kept being distracted. Water voles popped out of their holes to look at me, and swans came over and threatened me. So did a police launch. It cruised past and the officers eyed me suspiciously. I gave them my unsuspicious smile but they pulled over.

'Have you got a licence for that?' said one.

'For what?'

'That boat.'

'Er . . . well . . .'

'Right, you're nicked,' he said. Then his mate leant over and pointed to the pork pie sitting on my seat and said: 'What's that then?'

'My lunch. Want some?'

'Beneath it.'

Beneath it was a little blue sticker.

'That's my licence of course.'

I set off in the afternoon, sculling up through Windsor, catching a peek of the spires of Eton College through the trees. Some scholars loafed on the boathouse ramps but the river was too busy for them to take their fragile rowing boats out. All afternoon as the air thickened I picked my way through a milieu of boats: pedaloes, punts and cruisers, and ploughing a path through them all, a hotel boat with guests gazing down from the deck as if they were on a liner. The river was a playground and the splendid views of the castle supplied the classic backdrop. It grew smaller and smaller as I pulled my way westwards, then it was gone round a bend and instead a black cloud the size of a small European country filled the heavens, and suddenly all boats were running for cover. I wasn't really bothered. I just leant into the rain and felt the water refresh me. At one point a woman dressed in a coat and head scarf stuck her head out of a launch called *Maid Anita* and shouted: 'Are you enjoying yourself?'

'Yes thank you,' I shouted back.

'I should give up if I were you. We're going back to Datchet. Been a lousy trip all round. It's all right for him, he's been to sea. I haven't. We argue all the time. It all started in Marlow when I dropped the anchor over the side. Wasn't tied to the boat, see. People keep shouting at me.'

I reached Boveney lock as the rain intensified. The lock-keeper came out dressed in oilskins and sou'wester and, taking pity on the drenched duo that paddled into his chamber, he said I could moor for the night on his island. We sheltered in the gents' toilet. From the lock-keeper's cottage I could smell a roast dinner being cooked, which is a dreadful smell if you're not going to have any. I sat on the step and watched the vegetable patch fill with puddles. The cabbages had been gasping but now each leaf had a pond for the flies to dive in.

The rain stopped some time after dark but I spent a restless night as the weir stream roared. By the following morning the river had risen considerably.

As I packed up, the lock-keeper came and stood over me and shouted above the din: 'You should be all right. I'm not going to put the red flags up for the time being. Conditions aren't that dangerous, not yet anyway, not quite, almost though, could be by lunchtime. Travelling alone?'

'No, no. A girlfriend's joining me soon.'

'Dog's good company, I bet.'

'No, he farts too much.'

I cast off and felt the weir suck at me through its straw. And for the whole morning I battled against the wind and the current. My hands were raw and blistered and to those people who gave me waves of encouragement from the bank I apologize now for not waving back, the reason being that if I took my hands off the sculls for an instant I lost all the ground I'd made in the previous half hour. I particularly apologize if one of those waving to me was Vince Hill.

It took me four hours to reach Maidenhead, and I was rewarded with a town full of smooth edges that boasts a Pizza Hut, a McDonald's, a Kentucky Fried Chicken, and a Marks and Spencer's. It does have two fine bridges though. The first is one of Brunel's greatest hits, a railway bridge with two splendid arches incorporating the largest and flattest brick span in the world. Such an engineering feat was believed impossible when the bridge first opened, and Brunel was persuaded to leave his wooden structure in place to allay fears of collapse. Only when these supports were washed away in a flood a few years later was the great man able to admit they never reached the brickwork.

The second bridge is the town's, and is another graceful construction on which I am now an authority since I've been under it backwards, forwards, sideways and through every aperture. Each time I neared one of the holes or arches or whatever they're called, the current became so strong it swept me either downstream or clean through only to be picked up by another rush and thrown back through a different hole.

After four attempts I took a break and tried to call Jennifer. Her personal assistant answered.

'Jennifer Conway, please,' I said.

'Can I ask who's calling?'

'Personal call.'

'I'm sorry Ms Conway is busy.'

'It's Mark Wallington.'

'Oh, Ms Conway has gone to Brussels then.'

'What!?'

'That's the message she left.'

'Brussels! What the hell is she doing in Brussels?'

'She said she's sorry and that she would meet you later in the week. On Wednesday.'

'Wednesday?!'

'Hopefully. Personally I shouldn't think she'll make it.'

'Who are you?'

'Listen, you seem like a reasonable sort, you should steer clear of her, you know what she's like.'

I went back to the boat and thrashed my way under the bridge powered by raw aggression. I didn't need Jennifer's help or anyone else's to find the source of the Thames.

Not far upstream from Maidenhead I got lost. It was all the islands in the channel. They confused me.

5. Sonning. I'll Definitely Meet You in Sonning

Before Maidenhead the riverside had been tailored and well protected. It had been London's waterway and had had its edges clipped and every willow tree purposely placed. But as I headed up towards Cliveden, the east bank rose and grew into a cliff of beech and chestnut. Travelling backwards I hadn't noticed my approach, but now crags unfolded one after the other and the river was suddenly let loose. A mist crawled up into the woods so that the trees smoked and stood so still they appeared drugged. The river was a groove and I sculled slowly through the deep feeling heady, feeling for the first time the opiate of the river, and how it intoxicated all that it came into contact with.

At the top of the cliff among the trees stood the Italianate mansion Cliveden House. It was huge and loomed magnificently out of the mist and was impossible to look at without seeing a haze of scandal. For Cliveden had a reputation. If duels weren't being fought between dukes and jilted lovers in the gardens, then young women like Christine Keeler were being introduced to Ministers of War by the swimming pool, and it seemed to me to be more than mere coincidence when, passing the river frontage, I dipped my scull into the water and pulled out a sodden diary. I peeled the pages back in the hope I'd find material with which I could blackmail at the very least a member of the Cabinet, but the entries were clearly in code: 'Jan 1st. Dear diary. Got up late. Boring day. Anne Diamond is back on *Breakfast Time*. Arranged to meet Ben down the pub but the head gasket on his Toyota has blown. Started the jigsaw of the Matterhorn this afternoon. Think I'm getting a cold. Peter Snow chaired *Newsnight*.' At least I presumed the entries were in code. I didn't want to believe that someone's life could be so dull.

That night I sat in the boat in the lamplight and began my own diary. I wanted it to be an introspective and poetic account of the journey, but that didn't last very long. Instead I wrote about the wildlife I'd seen so far. My knowledge was scant but anyone who spent more than a few days on the river would soon have become intimate with all the creatures that lived on the banks, particularly the birds. I spent a long time each day just watching them paddle and scoot and swoop about their business.

Mallards, of course, were ubiquitous, but I'd never really noticed what beautiful birds they are, and how aerobatic. They left the water like jump jets and flew low and in formation, masters of their art. The males were recognizable by their beautiful blue-green iridescence, and their yellow grained beaks. The females, by the way they normally had three males on top of them. They were gregarious creatures but it was noticeable how they didn't get on with great crested grebes. I saw one have a fight with a grebe on one occasion and the grebe flattened it.

Canada geese were another common bird, although not so exciting to observe. They were awkward creatures that waddled everywhere with their noses in the air. They'd march along the banks or paddle on the water giving their young lessons in how to be supercilious. They mixed well with all the birds except the great crested grebes. I remember seeing a grebe mug one once.

Coots and moorhens were intriguing. They scurried about the riverbank and built their nests precariously among the reeds, or in empty burger boxes wherever the willows stroked the water. I liked coots and moorhens, I couldn't tell them apart but I felt we had a rapport. Great crested grebes didn't like them though. They picked on them and pecked them severely.

Herons were the most mysterious birds on the river. They were loners that stood for hours on logs at the water's edge, or by the weir streams. They were sad, silent fishermen, tall and sharp, skin and bone. Standing they reminded me of Fred Astaire in top hat and tails, and in flight their giant wingspan had a Wright brothers' design. Despite their size however they appeared timid birds – great crested grebes would beat them up regularly.

In fact great crested grebes were a generally violent bunch. They had a snarl on their beaks and a scar on their faces and they shuffled over the water with 'oi! are you looking at me?' expressions, shouldering everything else out of the way. Only one group of birds frightened them, the same one that frightened me – the swans.

In the short time I'd been on the river I'd already come to regard swans as remote and intimidating creatures. They knew their own strength and I always gave them a wide berth. Only occasionally would they try and charm, and then they'd paddle up to the boat, lean over the side and see what you had to offer. But their arrogance would prevail and they'd nudge you with an 'I'm beautiful aren't I? How about some of your lunch? Come to think of it, how about all of your lunch? Or the boat goes over, get it?'

But swans can afford to behave badly. Since the time of Richard I their population has been largely royal pro-

perty and highly valued. When in the middle ages the
king wanted to show his appreciation to the trading guilds
and city companies for their part in the military rearma-
ment, he ceded to them the privilege of keeping swans on
the Thames. Two guilds – the vintners and the dyers –
still exercise that privilege today, and join in the annual
Swan-upping ceremony when the swans are counted and
marked by the Queen's official Swan Keeper. Captain
Turk of Cookham is the current incumbent of this position. I had an image of the swans with some sort of
homing instinct that led them all to Cookham every July,
but the truth is Captain Turk sets off from London Bridge
in a ceremonial barge and heads upstream gathering the
birds. It's a splendid and historic custom but of note pri-
marily because the swan-keepers manage to do it at all.
Pictures and engravings throughout history depict the
swan-keeper of the time casually branding the birds with
a brush or knife, while the swan just lies there like a dog
having its belly tickled. My own experience of the birds
was quite different. If I got anywhere near one, it came
hurtling down the river, running on the water, wings
wide, like wild white horses with hooves flying, and anything but mute. They could hiss like snakes, and the beat
of their wings was a clamour. The idea of grabbing hold
of one and writing on its beak with a felt-tip 'this bird
belongs to the Queen' didn't seem like much of a job to
me.

But Cookham is clearly proud of its role in the ritual.
There's even a pub called the Swan-upper. I leant at the
bar, and asked the barmaid what she knew about the
ancient custom and she said: 'I don't really know anything
about it. Stan does but he's not in tonight.'

Cookham looked lovely in the night time. Its moor was
a spread of buttercups lit by the moon, and the floodlights

from the parish church cast long shadows around the village.

And the next morning there was still a general yellowness. The village was lush and surrounded by rape fields and the buses were painted marigold. It was another beautiful day but you got the impression it was always a beautiful day in Cookham. It was such a reassuring sort of place: it had cottages covered in roses, there was a flintstone church by the river, and the local curry house had exposed timbers.

I'd stopped in the village to visit the Stanley Spencer Gallery. I liked his pictures for their irresistible wickedness, and for the way he never let the gravity of his subject matter smother his sense of humour. He painted the Last Supper with the apostles playing footsie under the table.

Throughout the first half of this century Spencer was a familiar figure in Cookham pushing the pram that contained his artist's tools through the streets. He incorporated many village scenes in his work including the Swanupping ceremony and the Cookham Regatta. In his best known painting, *The Resurrection, Cookham*, he depicted a number of local villagers – himself and his wife among them – rising from their graves on Judgment Day, while the Thames slips by in the background. The gallery in the converted Methodist chapel where the painter used to worship houses a small but important collection of his work and I'd long wanted to visit it.

But it was shut. So I went to the churchyard to see if I could find Spencer's gravestone. I asked a woman if she'd seen it, and she said: 'Are you a visitor?'

'Yes.'

'So am I. Are you on the river?'

'Yes.'

'So am I. Who's Stanley Spencer?'

'A local artist.'

'No, I don't know him. We went to the Cookham Tandoori. George Harrison eats there and so does Vince Hill, or so I've heard. You know, him who sang "Edelweiss".'

The current had eased and the day warmed, I took my shirt off and sculled past the cliff edges of Cookham Dean Woods. The river began to meander, and the accents to thicken. At Bourne End I saw some cows in the river watering and heard some folk on the bank talking about tractors. There were hills in the background for the first time.

But I was entering a different phase of suburbia, that was all. The indiscreet chalets that had lined the bank downstream had now gone and been replaced by big houses in the pavilion style with windows thrust open to let in the spring. The residents sat in their garden furniture with their guard dogs at their feet, gazing at the water. I waved and said hello and they waved back to me with their teaspoons or celery sticks dunked in dip.

There was a sense of display here, though, that was unsettling. Because the trippers who passed in boats took photographs of these riparian owners the same way they would have of Dogon tribesmen in their mud-brick villages. If the locals were true natives, they would soon be forced to capitalize on the business potential here: 'We members of the Residents' Association have decided that each photograph takes away a little bit of our soul and so from now on, in line with the recent rate increases in the area, we've decided to charge a fee of 50p a snap. Cheques accepted with a banker's card only.'

As I passed one house I commented on the charm of the garden to the couple sitting in deckchairs on the lawn. In return they commented on the charm of *Maegan*. A rapport was established and their dog, an athletic-looking boxer, trotted down to the water front.

'He's been on TV, you know,' said his proud owner. 'He advertises a chain of hardware stores. He's the dog in the back seat of the station wagon that belongs to the chap who buys the loft insulation material. We're hoping to get him a role in the next series of *Juliet Bravo*. He was chosen for the glossiness of his coat.'

At this point Boogie appeared from under the covers and from then on relations went rapidly downhill. In my antique boat it was possible for me to melt into the scenery but Boogie stood out like a blot on the landscape. He has never been on TV, and he couldn't give a toss about a glossy coat – the more congealed the better as far as he's concerned. The couple in the garden took one look at him and called their TV star to heel – 'Come here, Bergerac.'

It was typical, really, of the culture shock Boogie was experiencing. Surrounded by all these pedigrees he felt insecure. For the rest of the morning he took his role as a passenger very seriously and lay on the back seat in protest. At the Marlow lock the keeper took a long look at him and said: 'Either that dog's dead or he's been doing all the rowing.'

His assimilation problems came to a head in Marlow, a pretty, neat, tidy, well-swept, parking-allowed-for-thirty-minutes-no-return-within-an-hour, thirty-five-minutes-from-Paddington, Georgian, brick and flintstone sort of place, with a Bejam, a Victoria Wine shop, a Waitrose, an Anglian Window Centre and an assortment of designer pedigree dogs, I tried out a few of the town benches, put some litter in the litter bins, sampled a zebra crossing and read some menus in restaurant windows, while Boogie made an effort and introduced himself to a red setter, a blue poodle, a labrador and, hardest of all, an afghan. They ignored him to a dog, wouldn't even point him to the local tandoori or the betting shop. He walked back to the river in disgust, only to find the boat surrounded by swans. Boogie doesn't know much about other animals except what he's picked up on *Wildlife on One*. When he sees something he's not familiar with, like a sheep, say, he doesn't chase it, he tries to nut it. I put him on his lead. I knew he wouldn't take to anything with a long neck and flat feet. Sure enough, with a 'red setters, afghans, swans, they're all a bunch of wankers,' shrug, he lunged at the birds. This moment of rashness coincided with the moment his lead snapped. He turned to me and gave me his 'I don't believe it, what sort of lead is that? I only lunged at these things because I knew you'd pull me back,' expression. I feared for the worst, but it only took a hiss, and a clout from a wing tip, and Boogie was cowering in the bottom of my shopping bag. Buses on the Wandsworth Bridge Road he could cope with, swans would take time and a complete rethink.

That afternoon I just dabbled slowly upstream, the river was in no hurry and neither was I. At Hurley lock the keeper, with an uncharacteristic display of officialdom, waited until I'd almost reached his gates, then looked at his watch, and hung up his Gone to Tea sign. The hydraulic locks on the Thames can be operated manually and the public are allowed to take charge when the keeper is off duty, but after an earlier attempt, when I left the river severely depleted and me severely exhausted, I elected to wait until the lock-keeper came back on duty. If the lock-keeper had a tea break, then so should I.

A few cruisers motored up to join the queue, I watched in horror as two adult coots or moorhens or whatever they were swam out of the reeds with their family of chicks, intent on giving them the hardest lesson of their lives – how to cross the river during rush hour. The adults headed off into mid stream, leading their family to what looked like a certain and very messy death as the brightly coloured hulls of the cruisers bore down on them like threshing machines. Used to the safety of the bank the chicks followed innocently, only to find themselves in heavy seas and having to paddle like riverboats just to keep their heads above the waves. They reached the other side somehow and had a roll call, but they would never have the same confidence in their parents again.

Presently, a beautifully decorated narrowboat pulled up. The man at the helm looked over at me and said: 'It's all right for the dog, isn't it?'

I smiled and he asked if I wanted a drink.

'I'll have a glass of champagne please.'

'I've got a cold beer,' he said and handed me a hot one.

'You know who you remind me of? *Three Men in a Boat*. My favourite bit is when they can't open the tin of pineapples. I'd love to do what you're doing and re-create their trip.'

'I'm not actually re-creating their trip, I'm just . . .'

'I mean the river's not really changed at all in a hundred years, has it?'

'I wouldn't be too sure . . .'

'I mean it may have motorboats on it and motorways over it, and the banks may be all privately owned, and most of the land developed, and all the commercial traffic may have gone, and the towns themselves changed unrecognizably, and of course all the mills disappeared, and there may be a fraction of the amount of wildlife there once was, and it might be impossible to find a mooring half the time, but it's not really changed.'

'Well, I think you'll find that . . .' But my point was lost as the lock-keeper opened the sluice gates and approximately eighty thousand gallons of water rushed off towards the North Sea.

The biggest Maid I'd seen joined us in the lock, *Maid Enormous* or something. It was like a bungalow. A man dressed in a suit leant out of the window and said: 'Tell us if we're going to squash you.'

They motored away and I was left to paddle out. The lock-keeper leaned on his gate, smoking, and I threw my eyes up in an 'honestly, the things that true watermen like you and me have to put up with, eh?' fashion, and he nodded and looked at my freshly sunbathed body and said: 'You're red, aren't you?'

Hurley was surrounded by chalk cliffs and dark islands where herons with beady eyes kept watch on the weirs. I paddled out of the lock cut to find I had the river all to myself. The flat calm returned and with it the acoustics lost on the winds of the previous two days: I could hear cuckoos everywhere. I leant back and thought about the most enjoyable thing I could think of. The truth was that when Jennifer did finally arrive it would be the first time we'd actually spend a night together, alone, in the same room as it were. It would have to be handled carefully. I couldn't be presumptuous. We were travelling companions, that was all. When she said she'd come on a journey with me nothing was implied. The important thing was to be reasonable. The river was good for being reasonable. It was soothing, and suitable for thinking things over. Since I'd made that phone call to Jennifer in Maidenhead, I'd realized my anger was simply directed at our different approaches to the journey. Mine was methodical, regimented. Hers was spontaneous, impulsive. But then Jennifer had always been an unpredictable sort. She'd made that clear from the start. We met by accident – a road accident that is. She knocked me off my bicycle. I was cycling to Italy, following the path of the first Roman legion to reach Britain in 55 BC, and I'd got as far as Blackheath and the start of the A2 when she reversed into me. I fell off and she insisted on buying me a drink. We went to a cocktail bar near the Blackwall Tunnel and she bought some champagne and said how she could easily fall for a man who cycled all the way to Italy. I explained to her that since my front forks were now bent beyond repair and my pedals made a noise that suggested a cracked bearing case, I would probably have to abandon the trip. But she said that such talk spoiled the romance of it all and she loaded my bike into the back of her TVR and took me to an Italian restaurant in Leytonstone where we had artichokes and garlic butter, and she got into a heated discussion with the waiter over the political role of the Catholic Church in Italy's social reform as a result of the unification. Over the zabaglione I said to her: 'Wouldn't it be funny if we got married because you knocked me off my bike?' And she laughed and said we must stay in touch. She gave me her phone numbers and we arranged to go out the following Wednesday, and that was the last I saw of her for six months.

'It's a contemplative thing the river is,' I said out loud, and I saw myself climbing up a slippery slope until it disappeared into the ground. 'A bit like life really,' I added, and a lone canoeist whistled past me.

'Pardon?' he said.

'Nothing. Nothing.'

A mile upstream I moored by the most beautiful house I'd seen on the river so far, Medmenham Abbey, a jumble of architecture, four hundred years old, standing in cool gardens. But its peaceful present disguised its decadent past, for here during the eighteenth century the Hell Fire Club met, that infamous, dissolute and ultimately rather silly band of men who under the aegis of Sir Francis Dashwood dressed up as monks and had get-togethers

every Wednesday under the motto: *Fay ce que voudras* —
do whatever you want.

To join the Hell Fire Club two qualifications were
needed: 1) to have been drunk, 2) to have been to Italy.
Meetings contained a variety of agenda, but virgins and
satanic rites and the perverse things you could do with
them seem to have been the most popular. Afterwards the
gang would repair to the Dog and Badger in Medmenham
village to unwind after a hard night's decadence. The pub
has changed rather since those days. Now there are no
cabals sitting in corners discussing whether or not to give
the holy sacrament to an ape next week. Instead the pub
is popular with RAF sorts sitting down to gammon steaks
with pineapple rings. I sat at the empty bar. The barman
said: 'It's always quiet on a Tuesday.'

I said: 'So what's all this about the Hell Fire Club?' and
he said: 'I don't know anything about it.'

From somewhere Boogie came back with a half a fish-
burger with garnish and tartare sauce. A man in a suit sat
next to me and said: 'Huh, the dog's got the right idea.'

I recognized him from the big blue boat which shared
the lock with me that afternoon. We sat in silence for a
while then I said: 'Saw you on the river today.'

'What?'

'I saw you on the river today. We were in the lock
together.'

'I haven't been on the river in twenty years.'

'You remember, you were in that big boat. I was in
my camping skiff.'

'In fact, I haven't been on the river since Macmillan was
Prime Minister.'

'And you said to me: "Let us know if we're going to
squash you."'

'I can tell you an interesting fact about the river,
though.'

'I'm sure it was you.'

'Herons eat ten thousand fish a year. Each.'

I found a phone box and left a message on Jennifer's answering machine for her to meet me in Sonning the following evening, then I took Boogie for a walk along the river towpath. A mist was down over the meadow. It swirled around my knees, and around his ears. It was a crisp cool night. I said: 'I'm glad in some ways Jennifer has given me a couple of days on my own.'

Boogie sniffed and clicked his tongue.

'And that's not to say I'm not missing her. I am. It's just that a trip like this is a time to be on one's own. That's the big difference between Jennifer and me. She doesn't like her own company. She doesn't like to be on her own for any long periods. I think that's why her poems are all so short.'

An owl coughed. Boogie turned and walked back to the boat. I spent the evening with Delia Smith. We cooked a delicious thick celery soup with smoked bacon. Afterwards I read her biographical notes and discovered that she lives in Suffolk and is married to the writer Michael Wynn-Jones. I also learnt her opinion on microwaves.

Next morning I planned to rise early, have a swim and get some sculling done before breakfast. Instead, I overslept. I pulled back the tent flap to see a fish jump out of the water and return with a plop. Above there was a vast sky crossed with the trails of aircraft. In the trees a rookery made a noise like a main-line station. The day had left without me again.

I made ready for departure as quickly as I could, but this process was taking longer and longer each day, not because of the tent dismantling, or any routine I had to go through, but simply because of my knots, a department of watermanship in which I had become particularly expert. I might even go so far as to say my knots were the most secure in the history of river navigation. Certainly they were the most original. The problem was they weren't the sort you'd find in any knot compendium and they could never be repeated or learnt. They were in fact different every time, and, rather than having any method, were simply the tightest jumble of rope I could manage. And so the measure backfired, because the disentangling of the trees, pillars, irons, stakes, gateposts, fences and cattle legs that the knot incorporated took hours the following morning. The strategy was successful in so far as I hadn't as yet drifted over any weir streams in the middle of the night, but it also meant that some mornings I wasn't on the water until midday.

The knot that secured me to Medmenham was a particular devil. I was keen to get moving but the knot was keener on me staying put. At one point I lost my temper with it and some walkers on the towpath made a detour around me. I didn't calm down until I reached Hambleden lock where the sun was shining off the lock-keeper's hat badge. He left his carrot patch to tend to me and say: 'Morning.'

'Morning.'

'All right for the dog, eh? Heading up towards Pangbourne?'

'Yes.'

'Make sure you call in at the Swan, best pub on the river.'

'Are all the pubs on the river called the Swan?'

'No, not all. There's the Trout at St John's Bridge. Then there's the Trout at Tadpole Bridge, and the Trout at Godstow. Not to mention the Perch at Binsey although I think they're going to rename that the Swan.'

This desire to conform was clearly part of the Thames ethic, and nowhere was it better expressed than in Henley, the town that lay just upstream from Hambleden at the end of the most famous mile on the river. My own performance along this the regatta course was unimpressive, hampered by my stopping halfway to feed some Winalot to the ducks. During the first week of July though, folk dressed in wellingtons are fenced off, and this part of the river is a rush of wood on water as very muscular people in very thin boats compete for silverware.

Of the many regattas held along the Thames, Henley's has always been the most popular, the rowers attracted by the long stretch of straight water, and the spectators by the town's facilities. As the halfway point by road and by water between Oxford and London, Henley was an important staging post long before the regatta was initiated and it could cope with the annual influx, one that increased greatly in 1851 when the regatta was given its royal cachet and became internationally renowned. Henley Week quickly grew to be the most popular date in the river's calendar with special trains from Paddington decanting spectators in the middle of the town from where it was a short distance to the riverbank and the lines of houseboats and barges. Elsewhere slipper launches, skiffs, punts and gigs fought for space and the river was a jam for a mile each side of the town. The whole affair was the biggest excuse for a picnic anyone had ever seen and somewhere among it all there was even time for some rowing.

For Henley was a place to be seen more than anything else. The crowds that fell off the train were nothing if not dressed in the latest river fashions. Men came in boaters and white flannels, blazers and canvas shoes; ladies, in laced hats, basqued bodices, serge skirts and mousquetaire gloves, all under a Japanese parasol. There is a feeling today that professionalism has crept into Henley's make-up, that the rowing has become too competitive and that the marquees are all public-relation tents for multinational companies. That may be so but nothing can change the image Henley acquired during the 1880s of the biggest annual festival of posing in the country.

I was almost two months early for the regatta but a grandstand and some marquees were already erected and the town was in a state of preparation. It was probably always so. There was a certain way of doing things in Henley – the regatta way – and everyone complied. Accordingly the town was a neat, well-organized, prosperous, meticulous, antiquified sort of place with a branch each of the Portman, Abbey National, Anglia, Halifax and Woolwich building societies, and a number of No Fishing, No Swimming, No Mooring, No Dogs, No Parking, No Ball Games signs.

Jennifer was arriving that night so I sacrificed half an hour of my life for her in Waitrose then lugged my groceries back to the boat and left town under the fine stone bridge which bore masks of the gods Thames and Isis. As I emerged I found an empty chocolate fingers packet had landed in my lap. And as Henley disappeared bit by bit behind willows, it occurred to me that most of the Thames towns and villages I'd stopped in had all been pretty and pleasant and historic, and yet despite – or maybe because of – their preservation societies they all looked strangely similar. I'd only been going a week but I was already having difficulty remembering one town from another.

'Backwaters!' said Mark Edwards, picking wood shavings out of his hair. 'They're great fun. You'll have a fine time exploring backwaters. Thanks very much, mine's a pint of Websters.'

Those were his very words as we sat in the pub in Hampton that first night. I remembered them well as I veered off the main channel a mile or two past Henley, and entered the darkness of Hennerton Backwater.

Although, it wasn't solely Mark Edwards who convinced me to take this diversion. A man I met just outside Henley helped as well. He was sitting on the bank on a stool, a duffel bag by his side. I said: 'Picnicking?'

'What's it to you?'

'I . . . I was just thinking what a nice day it was for a . . .'

'Ah shutup! Who cares? Clear off, you're disturbing the fish.'

'But . . .'

'But what?!'

'But you're not fishing.'

'Course I'm not! It's close-season, and it's a good job it is 'cos if it wasn't your boat would be just where my line would be.'

At other times of the year the banks of the Thames would have been lined with dark green and dour characters like this. The close-season had kept them indoors but this fellow was getting in a bit of practice at being abusive before the new season began. I said:

'What fish would you be fishing for it it wasn't close-season?'

'Chub! Now clear off.'

'Would you have had any luck? . . .'

'You're heading for trouble, you are, son.'

Fishermen were the most unpredictable creatures of the river and I knew they should never be underestimated. I'd heard stories of the most hardy oarsmen found in the bottom of weir streams or hung from willow branches by fishing line after they'd had the nerve to nod a greeting to a fisherman. But I took objection to this man's attitude and I said: 'On the contrary, I am heading for Cricklade.'

'Huh, not in that tub you're not.'

'Why not?'

'Too bleeding wide, you stupid git.'

'No she's not.'

'Listen, trout-face, you'd be lucky to get through Hennerton Backwater in that old pile of woodworm let alone Cricklade, now push off or I'll bombard you with maggots. And don't call in at the Swan in Pangbourne, 'cos, that's where I live and I don't want your sort there.'

So I thought I'd better test *Maegan* through Hennerton Backwater.

The opening was off the main channel through a veil of weeping willow. It was about fifty yards wide to begin with but very shortly tapered off to a slim cut. The water thickened and darkened to a slime and the vegetation formed a shroud so that only needles of sunlight pierced the foliage. There were no other boats. To begin with I was piloted through the undergrowth of fallen trees by a family of Canada geese, but after a way they disappeared and I was left with the nibbling insects. The birdsong sounded different here, and there were strange scuffling noises among the reeds. A couple of large water rats dived in the water with a sickly splosh.

After a few hundred yards the stream narrowed so badly I kept hitting the banks with the sculls and at each stroke I pulled a few pounds of weed out of the water. So in classic style, dressed barefoot and in shorts, I stepped up to *Maegan's* bow and began to paddle. I could have been travelling through the central American rain forest if it hadn't been for the sound of a lawnmower nearby.

Presently, I saw where the noise came from – a fine house set back a way through trees, with an extensive garden stretching down through orchards and coarse lawn to the water. All was peaceful until I saw the black head of a doberman peep through the willows.

Prior to this trip, if I'd been asked what the animal

synonymous with the Thames was, I'd probably have given the standard reply and said the swan or the duck. But my experience so far was steadily leading me to believe that these birds were heavily outnumbered by a different kind of wildlife – the alsatian or doberman guard dog.

On the river proper they weren't a problem. Boogie would sit in the boat posing like a pedigree, and stick his tongue out at the heavies, safe in the knowledge he was out of their range. The dogs could race through gardens to the water's edge and bark all they wanted – we were in mid stream and could pass with impunity. Down Hennerton Backwater though, the banks were a lot closer and this killer was striding alongside us just waiting for us to come that bit too close he could leap aboard or even grab my paddle and pull us to the bank. I could see a low bridge ahead which would have provided safety but before I could reach it Boogie, in his typically tactful style, blew a raspberry at the beast and that did it – the thing was in the river and after us. And not for him any primitive stroke like the doggie paddle, this neanderthal was doing the crawl. He wanted Boogie badly.

There was a time in Boogie's life when he would have taken on the best of them. He was never particularly tough, not even in his youth, but he quickly learnt how to climb trees which was a distinct advantage. When he approached middle age and lost his speed he turned to diplomacy and learnt to negotiate his way out of trouble which is what he'd have done in this situation had his assailant not been so far beyond discussion. I had the feeling the doberman was a professional guard dog, partly because of its manner, but also because running through the trees after it was a security guard – a tubby breathless man who had one arm longer than the other. As he ran he shouted to us: 'He's not playing! he wants to tear your limbs off!'

Boogie was a model of composure. I'd like to say for a moment his hackles rose and he contemplated defence. But he knew the hopelessness of the situation, and so he turned to me and gave me his 'well, it's been a good life' look. 'Thanks for everything. I know I've not been easy to live with, but I want to tell you how I appreciate what you've done. And I'm truly sorry about that time I made a mess in the fruit bowl. One request, no pedigrees at my funeral. And if you want to have some sort of memorial for me, make it a seat on Crouch End Broadway outside Radio Rentals and have it inscribed: "To Boogie, who loved the view".'

We were almost at the bridge, five more strong paddles and I'd be under. But the guard was now shouting: 'Lie down and pretend you're a tree. The dog is a trained killer.' I turned and saw two paws on the back of the boat. I was standing right on the bow as far away from the stern as was possible and yet Boogie was behind me. The paws began to pull the rest of the dog up out of the water. I prepared myself for the first mauling of my life. Then suddenly, out of the reeds dived two great crested grebes, and like the cavalry, swam towards the dog. They didn't look as though they had any intention of intervening, but their effect was immediate. The doberman took one look at them turned and splashed back the way he had come, squealing. The grebes spat and swam slowly out of sight. The guard led the doberman away like a lamb. I turned and banged my head on the bridge.

Now gnats formed a cloud around us. From the woods on the bank came a noise half-human, half-double-decker bus. In the murk a supermarket trolley lay rusting, its wheels in the air. The vines curled themselves around my neck, the water bubbled and snapped and we reached another bridge, this one so low I had to lie down in the bottom of the boat to pass under. My nose scraped the roof; I tasted slime. But before I could stand up again there was a dull thud and I looked up to see we were back in civilization again. We were in a marina and we'd hit a cruiser named *Black Stockings*.

'Hello there?' said a man in a sunhat scrubbing his deck. 'Look, it's *Three Men in a Boat*. Dog's got the right idea.'

I imagined the upper reaches of the river would be like Hennerton Backwater only with less depth and ten times as long. It was a daunting prospect but I couldn't complain, so far this trip had hardly been an ordeal. It had been a sunny jaunt through a landscape that strained for perfection. Sonning, where I moored that evening, looked so perfect it had the feel of a working model. Even the telephone kiosks had preservation orders on them. Only the traffic lined up the road from the narrow bridge restored reality.

I'd told Jennifer to meet me in the Bull at eight. I was there on the dot, sitting in the corner, trying to look anonymous. It was the landlord's fiftieth anniversary and he was celebrating the occasion by embarrassing everyone. Boogie disappeared and returned with a salmon sandwich and some ardenne pâté on French bread. The landlord spotted him and staggered over. He said: 'What sort is he?'

'Albanian retriever.'

'I thought he was. Here, are you on your own? I'll have to get you fixed up.'

'It's all right; a friend is joining me any minute.'

'Tell you what, there's a PE student over there. She's got blond hair, like you; you'll get on fine. Hang on.' And he staggered off again.

'No, my girlfriend is joining me later, honestly.' Boogie

sighed and shook his head. 'She is!' I said. But he'd seen what I hadn't – a tall figure in black leather standing at the door holding his crash helmet in one hand and a carrier bag in the other.

'Hello,' he said.

'Oh no!'

'Me again.'

'I don't believe this!'

'Mexican tonight.' He handed me the bag.

I said: 'I'm angry now. I'm being taken for granted.'

The messenger nodded. 'I think you should be angry.'

The landlord staggered back over. 'Her name is Sandra. She's from Andover. Nice place Andover.'

The motorcyclist messenger looked at me, sincerely, and said: 'You shouldn't be afraid of your anger. If you really want this woman you've got to be constructive with your emotions . . .'

The landlord prodded him and said: 'Here, are you on your own? Can't have that; I'll get you fixed up.'

'That's all right thanks. I'm in a relationship. It's not perfect, but then every relationship is an exercise in compromise, isn't it?' He leant closer to me and said: 'I always say that you've got to fall out of love with someone before you can really learn to love them. Sign here, please.'

He strode out. The landlord said: 'Here, don't get depressed.'

'Who's depressed? I'm not depressed.'

'Go over and speak to Sandra. She's dying to meet you.'

Sandra was a pretty young woman in a Fred Perry shirt and track suit sitting with a friend also in a Fred Perry shirt and track suit. They both looked serious and cradled tennis rackets. I smiled at Sandra and gave her a little wave. She looked the other way, then said something to her friend and they left.

Boogie and I walked back to the boat along the tow-path, clutching the Mexican meal. Inside the bag was a card that read: ' "At least I have not made my heart a heart of stone, Nor starved my boyhood of its goodly feast, Nor walked where Beauty is a thing unknown." I've had to go to Bologna. I'm really sorry. But I won't be long.'

I said: 'You see, most men would have got tired of it all by now. But not me. I know Jennifer better than she thinks. She's frightened that she's getting close to me, it's unnerved her. She feels threatened so she's distanced herself, literally. Well if this is a challenge I'm ready for it. She can be as unreasonable as she wants. I'll show her. I'll not react. That's what I'll do.'

Boogie licked something horrible out of an old plastic bag and we strode purposefully back to the boat.

During the night the wind picked up. It rained hard and the current tugged at *Maegan*. Next morning, I sculled off with great effort. A man walking along the towpath, whistling tunelessly, stopped and screwed up his face and said: 'Strong current today.'

'Yep.'

'Strong wind too.'

'Yep.'

'No motor, eh?'

'Nope.'

He weighed up the facts.

'Going the wrong way, really, aren't you?'

'Yep.'

6. Sorry About That. Give Me a Ring From Pangbourne

For two thousand years the Thames had no equal as a trading route and communication link. With all but ten miles of its length navigable it was an artery leading straight to the country's heart, and the Romans, the Saxons, the Vikings and the Normans all quickly realized that control over the river was a prerequisite to control over the nation.

They also realized that to keep this vital channel open, strict regulation was essential, otherwise the river would flood in the winter and be reduced to shallows in the summer. The millers and the fishermen had by Saxon times found a solution to the problem with crude versions of the weir. These provided pressure for the millers' wheels, and a trap for the fish, but they also provided a dead end for the boatmen, since they were little more than barricades across the stream. So flash-locks were introduced i.e. weirs with removable slats which provided a 'flash' of water on which a boat could be ridden downstream or winched up. These kept the boatmen happy, who now, on a good day, could ride the same flash all the way downstream – although on a bad day they would probably drown – and they kept the fishermen happy since the fish were channelled as before. But now the millers had grievances because the flashes of water undermined their waterpower. They made extortionate charges for boatmen to ride a flash; or frequently, if water levels were low, they'd simply refuse to open their gates. The result was huge delays for the boatmen who took to ramming weirs for their entertainment.

Fortunately, in Italy, where the Renaissance was well under way, Leonardo da Vinci was working on the problem. While our boatman and millers were standing on weirs squabbling, Leonardo was taking a far more systematic approach to the far greater problems facing Italy's waterway network. This had to cope with rivers that fell three hundred metres in as many miles and da Vinci knew that the only device of any use would be one that operated independently of the weir stream and yet used a comparatively small amount of water. His solution was the pound lock. Two hundred years later in the middle of the seventeenth century, the British got to hear of it and started to convert.

This was a costly and slow process. The first pound lock on the Thames was introduced at Iffley in 1633 but not till 1938 was the last flash-lock replaced. By then all parties concerned were largely grievance free, but this was because they were all largely redundant. The country's rivers and canals had declined as commercial routes in place of the railways; the fish were victims of pollution or people brought them in frozen boxes anyway; and watermills had been a joke for a long time. But the locking of the river did see the creation of one role: that of the lock-keeper.

I think it was at Sonning lock that I realized my vocation in life was to be a lock-keeper. The keeper there didn't speak to me as far as I remember, but that morning as I rose up the granite walls a further five foot four inches towards the source, and surfaced into a world of trees, flowers and mist to see the lock-keeper bent over his gate, nodding and smoking his pipe, I knew that his was the job I'd always wanted. It was clear to me that a lock-keeper was a man who woke up in the morning and stood on his front porch scratching his belly, surveying his vegetable patch and thinking to himself: Life is good when you're a lock-keeper. Then he would dedicate the day to being helpful to people, chatting to them, advising them, forgiving them when they gouged chunks out of his newly painted lock doors. He'd spend his spare time weeding his herbaceous borders, oiling his hinges, patting his dog and painting everything diamond white and gloss black. Then at lunchtime he'd take a break in his cottage which would be a hundred-and-fifty-year-old flintstone building with bright curtains and a crammed larder. In the afternoon he'd potter in his fruit cage and shine the plaques that commemorated the flood of 1847 and the year when he won Best Kept Lock of the Year Award. Then he'd bottle some jam for sale to passing boaters and go and sit under his sycamores for his tea break. After that he'd check the flow of the weir stream and as the sun went down he'd top up the hydraulic fluid levels and count the boats that had gone through his chamber that day, then close his register and go in for his supper. In the evening with the weir rushing under the moonlight he'd read Arthur Conan Doyle stories until he fell asleep in his armchair, the world a better place for the day he'd spent.

And so at the Caversham lock where the keeper had freshly painted bollards, manicured flowerbeds and permed hair, I said: 'You've got the best job of the world.' And as luck would have it he replied: 'There's a vacancy if you want.' But then he added: Long hours and lousy money and you don't meet as many girls as you'd think.'

'Oh.'

'It's boring as well.'

'Oh. Garden looks nice though,' I said.

'I hate gardening. It's boring. Do you know your boat smells of roast dinners?'

As it happened I had noticed a faint smell of roast dinners all morning but I couldn't understand where it was coming from. In fact I couldn't understand a lot of things that morning. The most odd was Boogie's desire to help me out with the sculling. I should have guessed his behaviour and the smell were connected. His lassitude of the previous few days forgotten, he spent the morning trying to push me off the sculls and take over my position in the boat. He even started to lick the scull-chocks and that was when I made the connection. I'd greased the sculls before I set out from a tin I'd found in the bottom of the boat. The grease had come straight from a roasting tray, and now the sculls were like beef lollies.

We were approaching Reading. Gathering on the horizon were the gasworks, pylons, scaffolding and railway cuttings of the biggest city since London.

Some swans escorted us in, or rather made sure we kept to a certain lane. There were a large number of them on the approach. They'd found a refuge in a house on the bank where a man stood by his open back door and threw bread and vegetables for the birds and they clamoured around him. I'd seen similar scenes on a number of occasions since London. The houses were surrounded by swan dung and feathers, and the people who fed the birds had long necks and noses and walked with flat feet. When they died they'd have their ashes sprinkled over the river and for years afterwards the swans would come and expect to be fed.

We passed the river Kennet and the entrance to the

Kennet and Avon Canal. And for the first time I felt the river narrow noticeably. In London it had been an old and worn corrugated slab of water looking as though it expected to find the sea round the next corner. Here it was young and gritty and needed big gulps to swallow a river like the Kennet.

Reading was a town with a charm all of its own. As we slipped under the town bridge an empty Toblerone packet landed in the boat thrown by a lad who leant over the parapet with his tongue stuck out. I said: 'What's your name?!' And he shouted back: 'Nigel Leyton, aged twelve, what of it, Mister?'

And then by Caversham Bridge a gang of skinheads sat all over a bench, smoking and shouting and throwing things. I asked them what Reading was like and they were surprised to find someone addressing them. They were suddenly quiet as they tried to work out who was to be their spokesman. Finally, one said: 'It's got an inner ring road and an outer ring road.' And then another said: 'It's got a biscuit factory.'

I stopped in Reading briefly just to fill up with water, but Boogie saw a Pelican Crossing and had to have a go on it. Then he saw a car park and he wanted a run in that, and then we had to have a walk down the pedestrian precinct and have a look at the bus depot. Finally he wanted to lick some parking meters and visit the railway station redevelopment, and in the end it was a couple of hours before we could get away.

But, like all the towns it passed through, the Thames left Reading by a back door and within ten minutes I'd found an island in the stream and was sat on a branch of a low-slung willow, brewing up.

A coot paddled past me; a moorhen followed. I fancied I was finally able to tell the difference between them. It wasn't their paddle motion or the size or shape of their nests. And it wasn't their cry or their mating ritual, nor the size of their brood nor their defense tactics. The difference was that coots had a bright white head while moorhens had a bright red and yellow one. Birdwatching isn't easy but you get the hang of it after a while.

I snuggled into the tree sheltering from the warm drizzle. I liked these islands in the river. They'd been a feature all the way since Kew. The Saxon word for them was eyot and there was something dark and disturbing about them, except for when they had executive hotels and landscaped lawns such as on Monkey Island near Maidenhead, or when they had housing estates like one near Shepperton.

This particular one was just an overgrown lump of vegetation and didn't look as though anyone had set foot on it for years. Hardly had the thought left my head than a cloud of diesel called *Maid Ugly* appeared. Its wash climbed my boat. The coots and moorhens dived for cover and bits of bank fell in the water as the driver leapt out and tied up: 'Good place you've found here,' he said. 'Look, there's even a supermarket trolley.'

Sure enough a supermarket trolley was sticking through the mud on the bank; only an experienced eye would have spotted it. I said: 'I can't understand why people throw supermarket trolleys into rivers.'

'That's because you've never done it, have you?'

'Have you?'

'Yes, I have as a matter of fact.'

'What's it like?'

'Well, put it like this: now I think the world is divided into two sorts of people – those who have thrown supermarket trolleys into rivers and those who haven't.'

I greased the sculls again and Boogie licked them dry again and we headed up to Mapledurham. The sun came out and the river was a mirror. The reflections of Mapledurham House and the old mill were a shimmering water-colour, a pool of life that looked as though one could walk on it. I threw a stone and a shock of ripples hurried over the surface with a shiver then the water quickly returned to its mirage-like state. The river was made up of many things, but it was the reflections that gave it its extra dimension. It was easy to forget about them at times, to take them for granted and not notice them for long periods. But every now and again I'd see a special display such as this and then I could see the whole earth and sky in the water. The reflections were sharper at some times of the day than others but they were always there some-where, and in the evening as the dusk seeped into the edges of the landscape and the sun set, the reflections were left behind in the water for a short time, until the last of the daylight dragged them off into the woods.

The stretch from Mapledurham to Pangbourne was glo-rious, the sort of scene I'd pictured when, before I set off, I'd closed my eyes and tried to imagine the journey. On the bank stood old sycamores so colourful you could taste their sweet blossom. Insects skated on the breathless surface; fish shoved their faces through a ring of water; some horses came down to the bank to look at me; and there in the most splendid setting was Hardwick House, standing back from the water, its gardens sloping grandly down through vivid meadows. By the landing stage two herons stood motionless on a log, like guards, grinning and waiting.

The evening had become calm and warm. The only sound was *Maegan* breaking the water. I had the reach to myself and I spent hours exploring every creek. The river was a box of tricks and I crept about, frightened to move too suddenly in case I broke something.

At length I got to within sight of Whitchurch Bridge and I moored to watch some canoeists playing water polo.

I made camp and then walked along the towpath towards Pangbourne, preparing myself for a frank telephone conversation with Jennifer. Her behaviour was putting the expedition into jeopardy. It was time to be firm. Well, firmish.

Some other boats were moored for the night, but there was little activity from them. I'd hoped there might be some sort of boatman's camaraderie on these mooring sites. I'd thought there might be campfires at night and folk gathered together singing songs of the Thames, roasting fish on the fire and telling tales of ghost barges and house prices in Chertsey. Instead, most crews threw their slops out of the window, then pulled the blinds and switched on the television, and that was that.

As I neared the bridge though, I saw a different kind of boat. It was moored away from the others and looked put together out of orange boxes and rope. Its blue and white paint was peeling and faded. Washing hung from bow to stern. The windows were coated in grime and condensation, and lashed to the deck was an impressive display of paraphernalia: a bicycle, a fishing net, fenders, petrol cans, a mattress, a standard lamp, a Hoover. It looked like a tramp's steamer. But the most unnerving part of it all was the dog bowl on the bank outside. It was the size of a bucket and had the name Ralph written on it. Where Ralph was I didn't know but I didn't want to meet him, that was for sure, and I passed on tiptoe. Boogie, on the other hand, who is either fearless or stupid, but probably stupid, went over to the bowl and started to lick it out, tripping over a mooring line in the process. Like a spider sensing a touch on its web, a man came dashing out of the cabin. He had a tattoo on his arm and a snarl on his face, and he said: 'Get lost.'

'Sorry.'

'What's your dog doing?'

'Nothing.'

'Clear off.'

'Yes, we're going.'

'You were pulling up my moorings.'

'It was an accident.'

'Push off.'

Then he eyed my wellingtons. 'You've got wellingtons on,' he said.

'Yes.'

'You don't see many wellingtons on the river these days.'

'No?'

'You've got a stupid hat on as well.'

'Yes.'

'You don't see many stupid hats on the river these days.'

He eyed me meanly, then reached behind him and put his own hat on. It was really stupid.

'Where are you heading?' he asked.

'The source.'

'What sort of boat?'

'Camping skiff.'

'Like *Three Men in* . . .'

'I promised myself I'd hit the next person who said that.'

He sniggered. 'You can come in if you want.'

'What about Ralph?'

'Ralph? That's me.'

'You've written your name on this bowl?'

'It's my bowl isn't it? I write my name on everything that's mine.'

He had indeed. As I climbed down the steps into the cabin I found myself in a room that resembled a loaded removals lorry, only more tightly packed. You could pick something up to sit down but then there was nowhere to put down the thing you'd just picked up. Ralph had got round that problem by sitting down on the thing he would have picked up. In the end I held on to the thing I picked up – a picture in a broken frame – and I sat on a box that contained another box. Ralph handed me a cup of something. The cup had Ralph written on it. So did Ralph's cup.

'Where are you headed?' I asked.

'I'm not headed anywhere. I live here. Lived on the river for thirty years.'

'Bet you've seen it change?'

'Everyone asks me that.'

'What do you tell them?'

'I tell them it's changed.'

He gave me whisky with dust in it. I wanted to ask him so much but he liked silences. He'd asked me on board and now wanted to share a silence with me. I looked at the picture I had in my hands. It was of a medieval bridge across the river. The bridge was on piers and there were buildings and turrets and a chapel on it. Underneath, the caption read: Old London Bridge. Ralph looked at me and said: 'Do you believe in time travel?'

'. . .'

'If you could choose one period and place in history to go back to where would it be?'

'. . .'

'If, say, you could go on your holidays to the period of your choice; if you could just walk into a time-travel agent and flick through a brochure of periods in world history and pick the one you wanted to visit most, where would you choose?'

'Ancient Greece.'

'Good choice. You know where I'd go? I'd go back to London when that bridge was there.'

I looked at the picture again – stalls and carts and horses, grand houses several storeys high jutting out over the water, boats and mist and flags. All life seemed to be going on.

'Lasted over six hundred years that bridge did. The city was a skyline of spires and belfries in those days, and as cosmopolitan a place as you could find in Europe. Traders from all over settled in London, and the bridge was its pulse. Ravens flew among the turrets, and decapitated heads hot from the Tower were stuck on poles at the bridge gates. Here, hold this a minute.' He handed me a box, then another box, then a typewriter and then a sewing machine and he burrowed down into his belongings. With surprising speed he was at the bottom of the pile, emerging with another picture, an engraving this time. It showed a frozen river and in the background the same bridge.

'The bridge used to slow the river down, see, and it would freeze, and then everyone would take to the ice and great frost fairs were held. Winter celebrations with oxen roasting on the ice. There were bear fights, bull-baiting, games and market stalls of all sorts. You could drive a coach and four over the river.'

I could recall the Thames freezing over in my lifetime but never in London, always upstream. I said: 'When was the last frost fair?'

'Beginning of the nineteenth century, just before they knocked the old bridge down. The new one hadn't the number and thickness of supports and the water wasn't dammed like it had been. They built embankments as well and so the river was narrower and faster and couldn't freeze.'

He seemed sad. He filled his glass and said: 'But what a sight it must have been. I've lived and worked on the river for years and I miss that bridge even though I never saw it.'

'You worked on the river?'

'Yes.'

'Doing what?'

'All sorts.' He didn't want to talk about it, but he was the first waterman I'd met; someone who could actually tell me something about the old commercial river.

'What sort of work?' I asked.

'Towing. We towed barges down from Lechlade to Reading.'

He was silent again.

I said: 'I bet you've seen it change?'

'Everyone asks me that. In fact you've just asked that.'

'Ever been further upstream than Lechlade?'

'Once. Wish I hadn't.'

'Why?'

'Let's talk about London Bridge some more.'

'Have you ever found the source?'

'No. But I met someone who did.'

'Where is it?'

'It's by a tree.'

'Any particular tree?'

'Can't remember. But the tree had TH written on it, or so I was told.'

'TH?'

'TH.'

'What does TH mean.'

'I don't know, maybe Thomas Hardy went there and carved his initials, how should I know. I'm going to bed now. You be careful going to the source. You'll lose all your spoons.'

I left Ralph and walked round Pangbourne looking for a telephone. They were all broken so I went into a hotel and put mud on the carpet and asked to use a phone. As Jennifer's number rang I rehearsed my speech: 'This is getting ridiculous. You're being unreasonable. I'm not prepared to take any more of this. If you're not here by the weekend . . .' The answering machine came on: 'This is Jennifer Conway. I'm sorry I'm not able to take your call but leave a message and I'll get back to you. And if that's Mark, I know what you're thinking. You're thinking: this is getting ridiculous. She's being unreasonable. You're not prepared to take any more of this. If she's not there by the weekend . . . Well, I've got good news and bad news. The bad news is I've got to go to Oslo. The good news is I'll be back by Tuesday. Promise. Did you visit Reading Gaol? Of course you did. It's where Oscar Wilde was imprisoned. That's why I sent you that Oscar Wilde quote. I would have sent you lines from the *Ballad of Reading Gaol* but I discovered he wrote that in Paris not Reading but then I'm sure you know that. Leave a message at the office where you'll be on Tuesday. I can't wait.'

I walked back to the boat, lit the lamp and began to prepare chicken in a paprika sauce. Tonight it would be me and Delia again. I looked at her picture on the cover of her book. How pleasant she appeared, standing there with her hands under her chin. She looked like a wholesome sort, good to travel with. Not the sort to let you down on an expedition to the source of a great river. She'd be there by your side doing her share of the paddling, no matter what. I sat in the shadows on the border of Berkshire and Oxfordshire and prepared chicken in paprika sauce and tried to imagine what it would be like to travel with Delia Smith. A journey across the Sahara would be more her forte. I could imagine her trading with the nomads for juniper berries to give her pepper steak piquancy. I could just see her bartering in the medinas of Tamanrasset for root ginger to give her stir-fried mange-tout that essential zest. She looked like a resilient woman, not the sort to be discouraged just because her brown kidney soup got full of sand. She knew the meaning of the word commitment – you only had to read her opinion on packeted Parmesan cheese to recognize that. By the same token though, you only had to read her section on tinned tomatoes to realize she wasn't the sort of woman who couldn't improvise if needs be. If we got caught short of food, for instance, she could probably rustle up something very nourishing from Boogie's Winalot. These things are important when you're considering a travelling companion.

Inside the tent, the paprika sauce simmered. Outside, the water lapped on *Maegan*'s mahogany, and the shrill song of the night birds pierced the dark. The noises of the night were so sharp I could even hear fish; I was sure I could. They made a faint pop when enough of them got together and broke the surface. Only the river was quiet. For such a large mass travelling such a distance at such speed it was a remarkably silent work of nature.

The chicken was wonderful. Tomorrow I would write a postcard to Delia and let her know. I lay back and made animal shadows on the ceiling. The lamplight shone on the Winalot packet. There was an offer on the back: fifteen tokens for a plastic dog bowl. Thirty tokens for a feeding mat. A hundred and twenty-five tokens for a giant wool-and-mixed-fibre blanket. On the side there was a chart recommending the size of meal to give each size of dog. It turned out that Boogie, who should have been eating the same amount as a corgi or a standard dachshund or a fox terrier, was putting away the recommended diet of a doberman. I cut out the coupons. At the rate he was going we'd have the mixed-fibre blanket before we reached Oxford.

Outside, an owl cleared its sinuses. Inside, Boogie came over and lay by me; he seemed to sense my solitude. He tried to climb in my sleeping bag; I seemed to sense his foul breath.

He looked at me sorrowfully. 'Don't look at me sorrowfully,' I said. 'She'll turn up. I know she will. You'll see.'

I turned the light off then turned it back on again and made a note on my mental state. I was concerned by the way I had taken it for granted that Boogie would be with me when I travelled trans-Sahara with Delia Smith.

The rains came again that night and the river rose and was far too fast for me to get up early and have a swim so instead I had a lie-in. But I was there at the gates of Whitchurch lock as the keeper came on duty. He looked at me with great concern as I rose up to his level, then said: 'What day is it?'

'Friday.'

'Bugger,' he said, then went back to his flowerbed.

The current was a struggle again, but I was better able to cope with the vagaries of the river now. I'd learnt how to feather my sculls, and I bent my knees and pulled with my body, and I never took my wellingtons off unless I had to. I had the vernacular as well. I used expressions like 'astern' rather than 'the back end', 'amidships' rather than 'that bit there'. I called the depth of *Maegan*'s water displacement 'the draught'; the extreme front of her the 'stem'; and the people who motored up the river at fifty miles an hour and disturbed the coots 'bastards'.

I pulled steadily away from the lock. The river felt thicker after the rain, and the sensation of being in the control of something powerful and inevitable grew stronger with each mile. The elixir-like flow drew all life to its banks. And not just wildlife – churches loved to hide in its recesses; the fine country houses that I passed were all possessive of their river views; the land and the farm stock all lurched towards the water for sustenance.

And I began to find something significant and something personal attached to each meander, nowhere more sad than at Basildon where I arrived mid morning. I'd stopped to see Basildon Park, a splendid Georgian mansion with, so I'd been told, an Ionic portico and strange octagonal-shaped rooms. I understood it to house a unique collection of Anglo-Indian objets d'art, as well as some fine frescoes and a garden of great design. Unfortunately it was closed, so I rested for a while in the local churchyard. I'd pulled against the strong current for three hours and wanted to rest in some shade, and here was a haven of trees, long grass and wild flowers, a miniature wilderness, untouched by Black and Decker edgers, where butterflies flourished and grass grew to four foot in places. Boogie had three different species of spider crawling over him.

I strolled around reading the gravestones. It's normally easy to distance oneself from these brief biographies, but there was one here that brought a lump to my throat and illustrated what a taker as well as a giver of life the river is. It was a memorial, a stone sculpture to two young boys, erected by their parents. An inscription told how the boys had drowned in a backwater nearby in 1886. The family had lived at the church farm at the time. The river had flowed past only a few hundred yards from their door and was an integral part of the local life, but it shouldered no responsibility. It couldn't be trusted. It acted imperviously and hurried on its way without a thought.

There was no one about in Basildon. The village and the fields were deserted. Only the rooks and the aircraft caught the eye; the only noise came from the hammers of the British Rail workers on the bridge downstream. I left feeling like a voyeur – my biggest fear when travelling. And in this case particularly unsettling, because with the ease of changing channels on a television, I went from the saddest part of the day to the most exciting.

For if Basildon was sad and silent the Goring Gap, a mile upstream, had the air of a celebration. This gorge is the place where the post ice-age Thames burst through the ridgeway formed by the Berkshire Downs and the Chilterns, then swallowed the river Kennet and continued east through its new valley. Before I'd set out everyone had told me this was the most impressive stretch on the river and I remember feeling a tension that was strange because it was so unlike the Thames. As the banks tightened and rose into cliffs I could sense the land choke so that approaching the gap was like being poured out of a bottle.

I entered the gorge and came upon the village. The postcards in the local shops were all pictures of the gap and of the lock, and Goring was undoubtedly a picturesque place, a fine example of what nature can do given beech trees and chalk cliffs. But the most compelling part of this village is something that could never be photographed – not unless Ralph's idea for time travel got off the ground – for above all else the village is an historic junction, the place where the two ancient trade, military and stock routes, the Ridgeway and the Icknield Way, linked up. Since stone age times news from the east met news from the west here, and as I walked round the village and its neighbour, Streatley, I had the feeling I was treading on a very worn and smooth pavement. I must have been looking very intense because as I towed *Maegan* into the lock a man with a briefcase saw me and said: 'Cheer up.'

'Sorry, I was ruminating on stone age man and the ice age, and thinking how insignificant in general we all are,' I said.

Then he saw *Maegan*: 'Of course, *Three Men in a Boat.* You realize, of course, that it was in Goring they stopped to get their clothes washed? They got a woman to do it in that pub over the bridge. I suppose you're re-creating the trip. It's a hundred years ago that Jerome wrote the book, you know?'

I asked him if he lived in Goring. He said he did and it was pleasant enough. He'd played for a pub darts team a number of years ago. But he was too tired most evenings now. He said: 'The best thing about Goring though, is it's handy for Junction 6 on the M4 and only thirty-five minutes from Paddington.'

It was a casual remark, but as I pulled away from the lock I realized he'd perfectly described the commuter-land ethos. To me Goring felt a long way from London. It had grown because of its role as a crossroads and was independent of the capital. That is to say it had a heritage. But now, like everywhere else the river had led me through, Goring had been revalued on the strength of its proximity with Paddington and the motorway, and I was sure the circling Boeings of Heathrow were a comfort to most folk rather than a disturbance.

There was, of course, a price to pay for this convenience. Commuter towns and villages had such a high desirability status that everyone wanted to live there, but by the time the commuters had purchased their property they had nothing left to spend, so the communities were dead. Not only did folk spend all day in London, they then came home and spent each night indoors. Something fundamental to the village had been lost. The community spirit was reduced to a Neighbourhood Watch sticker in every front window.

I sculled away through a sea of dandelion seeds. The gap soon disappeared and the river retained its composure after its brief fling. Ahead was Moulsford Bridge, a grand and angular span of red brick skewed across the water. I could see its elegant form from a distance, and yellow-nosed 125s flashing over. And I smiled when I thought that there was a man who could be held responsible for the creation of the commuter belt, our old friend Brunel, the man who never saw a hill without seeing a tunnel, never saw a river without seeing a bridge. His railway line had given all the Thames' towns and villages their high-speed link with the capital, and ultimately their convenience rating.

At yet, unlike the roads which crossed the river, the railway line seemed woven indelibly into its fabric. Part of this was nostalgia, but part of it was because the railways seemed under control whereas the roads were an impossible strain on the land. I waved to the passengers on the trains and they all waved back and I knew that, if anything, I found the railway lines reassuring. I remember them especially in the dark. I'd peer out of the tent some nights and see carriage lights tracing their way through the dark countryside and I'd feel a strange comfort.

Now I stopped under Moulsford Bridge and waited for an Intercity. I could feel the vibrations a long way off: the river began to crease as the train came over the adjacent field, pushing the air before it. The bricks began to roar, the whole bridge to groan, then the train screamed overhead and the river rattled.

I sculled long and hard that evening, almost reaching Wallingford. In the dusk I tied up under a high bank with the mist crawling over the fields towards me. A grebe paddled into a clump of reeds. There was a thump and a scream and an oof! and a duck limped out, winded.

I pulled out the canvas and struggled to tie the ropes which had shrunk in the rain of the previous night. Boogie was lying languidly in the long grass and I said to him: 'It's your decision of course, but I'd be really grateful if you could hold this end of the rope in your teeth because it would aid me considerably in securing the canvas. I'm not saying you have to, it's your right as a dog to refuse, you might for example prefer to be up in the village in the local pub right now, but if you could assist . . . Come back here!'

I decided to cook outside. I set the stove up and suddenly there was a greyhound standing next to me, eyes ablaze. It was a shock that made my heart jump. The thing pinned me to the boat, its face not two inches from mine. Out of the half-light its owner approached, a man whistling a tune tunelessly. He said: 'People are always terrified by my dog, can't understand it, myself.' It was the second most stupid comment I heard all night.

The most stupid came from the same gentleman but a little while later when it was dark and the railway was a distant flash and clatter. I was washing my dishes in the river. A spoon fell in the water never to be seen again – I was down to my last one. I sat there watching the ripples slowly iron themselves out when suddenly the greyhound was sitting next to me again. It was uncanny, like turning a light on and off. One minute he wasn't there the next he was. I called out for help to my faithful travelling companion who had come back from the pub now and was having his meal, but Boogie's a lousy guard dog at the best of times and with his nose in a bowl of Chum he's stone deaf. 'I've saved your life three times on this trip!' I screamed, but he put his paw over his eyes and continued eating.

The owner turned up again, whistling a different tune, although just as tunelessly. He called his dog away: 'He likes you,' he said. Then he looked at Boogie and said: 'How old is he?'

'Dunno.'

'He's getting on.'

'Yes.'

Then he looked stuck and he smacked his lips and said: 'They get old, dogs, don't they?'

And that was the most stupid thing I heard all night.

But it could well have been a crucial point in the journey as far as my mental state was concerned. Because the next day when I reached Wallingford a strange thing happened to me which left me rather unsure of the effect the river was having on my general condition. A woman walking along the towpath saw Boogie and said: 'What sort of dog is that?'

'Maltese spaniel.'

'Thought so,' she said, then skilfully changed the subject by giving me some indispensable piece of knowledge concerning *Maegan* and Victorian rowing boats in general, finishing with a lovely story of her grandparents who had gone on a camping skiff holiday on their honeymoon from Wallingford to Oxford and back.

Had I been fresh on the river I'd have joined in conversation with this delightful person on the whimsical joys and contemplative pleasures of the Thames. But it was as if having been on the water for a while I badly needed the bilges in my brain pumped out. I could feel myself becoming more the sort of person who walks up and down the towpath at nightfall, whistling tunelessly, and so I said: 'Huh; it's all right for a dog, isn't it? The dog's got the right idea.'

And she looked strangely at me and said: 'Travelling on your own?' And I thought of Jennifer for the first time that day and hurriedly said: 'No, no, a girlfriend's joining me on Tuesday. She was supposed to be starting the trip with me in London, but . . . well, she's a busy woman, and then she got delayed when I was in Hampton, and then in Windsor and then in Sonning, and then she had to go to Oslo or somewhere, but she's coming on Tuesday for sure.'

The woman nodded but looked as though she'd meant to shake her head, and said: 'Well, I hope so.'

7. I'll Wait for You outside Boots in Oxford

Next day I called Jennifer's office. Her PA answered.

'I'd like to leave a message for Jennifer Conway,' I said.

'Ms Conway is in Os . . .'

'I know she's in Oslo.'

'It's you again, isn't it?'

'Tell her to meet me in Oxford on Tuesday.'

'She won't be there.'

'That's her decision.'

'You really expect Jennifer Conway to go with you in your silly little boat up the Thames?'

'Yes.'

'You're nuts.'

'Just give her the message.'

'Listen. You must be meeting all sorts of nice girls, why don't . . .'

'Just tell her to meet me outside Boots at two o'clock.'

One thing this trip had taught me was that every town has a Boots.

It was Saturday, and the cruisers were out in numbers, I had a couple of near misses but generally other boats cleared a passage for me – it was an advantage of travelling backwards.

Near Benson though I collided with a very expensive-looking vessel and since it was stationary I had to take the blame. But the owners were very understanding. They leaned over the side, saw Boogie asleep on the back seat and said: 'Ah! poor dog. We didn't wake him did we?'

They asked me on board for a drink. I sat there on the hot plastic of the driver's seat before an array of levers and switches. Basically all these boats were very similar, but the owners always managed to express themselves in some way or another, usually in the choice of name. This is the most difficult decision a boat owner on the Thames ever has to make, needing the ability to sum up your past, your future, your bank balance, your politics, your sexuality, your marital status, your creativity, your childhood traumas and whether or not you've read *The Lord of the Rings*, all in one word.

The most popular nomenclature was the bucolic – names like *Burwood* and *Skylark II*. Then there was the naval – *Pompey Boy, Jolly Roger*; and the cute – *Dollydrop, Pretty Penelope*. Some were poetic – *Windrush, Zephyr*; and some were enigmatic – *Zagala*. Then there was the macho – *Hesoutonisownagain*. And the unashamedly sexist – *L'autre femme II*. The cost of these beautiful boats would, I'd have thought, made them the craft of the few, but that wasn't the case at all. Some of the most unlikely sorts were at the helm. I got the impression some boats were the spoils of crime, they should have had names like *Dunmuggin*, or *Brinxmat Job '84*.

The boat I'd collided with was called *Betibob*, a member of the domestic set, simply a combination of the couple's names, a symbol of their happy retirement. And they'd created that atmosphere perfectly. There was Bob on the deck with his arms folded, grinning, and there was Betty at the table putting hard-boiled eggs through the slicer.

I said: 'I saw an old Victorian houseboat downriver a

few miles back,' which was a complete lie but I was lost for conversation and so I thought I'd make something up. I had seen pictures of old Victorian houseboats though, and they looked the most splendid constructions, luxurious and stylish display cabinets in a fanciful game of oneupmanship played by the wealthy. I told Betty and Bob this, but they took it as a challenge to their own observation skills. Bob said: 'Mmm, I saw a hovercraft just below Wallingford Bridge.'

'Mmm,' I said. 'I found a supermarket trolley with six traffic cones in it in the backwater up by Shiplake.'

'We found a dead donkey in the weir by Boulter's Lock,' said Betty.

'Really,' I said. 'I found a frozen chicken in Pangbourne Reach.'

'We met someone who said they'd found a World War II mine in the marina in Reading,' said Bob.

'Yes,' said Betty. 'And they'd met someone who said they'd seen Lord Lucan in a narrowboat just past the Goring Gap.'

I sat back. I couldn't match that. The plastic seat stuck to the back of my legs and from the saloon came the smell of a hot television. Betty peered over at Boogie who was still asleep on *Maegan*'s back seat. She said: 'Doesn't the dog have a life jacket?'

'No,' I replied. 'The truth is he finds them more of a hindrance than a help. You see, he's highly trained as a life saver. Don't let that calm, dozy exterior fool you for a moment. He's constantly on guard. If any child, or any person for that matter, was to fall in the river now he would instantly dive in and haul them back to shore, administering kiss of life on the way if necessary. A life jacket would only slow him through the water, losing valuable seconds that could mean the difference between life and death.'

'Oh,' said Betty, and Boogie yawned, stretched, licked his lips, rolled over, farted and went back to sleep again.

The day grew hot then humid, gripped in a sweaty hand. As I sculled under the elegant Shillingford Bridge some sandwich crusts floated past me. I pulled my way through the sticky afternoon and into the evening until I reached the mouth of the river Thame. A low bridge prohibited larger craft access but I was able to scull up it to a sandbank and I moored there under a willow among the reeds.

Later I walked through the meadows into Dorchester, a pretty Oxfordshire village crammed with cottages, coloured with wisteria, and all wrapped around its abbey.

And there was a concert in the abbey that night – concertos and cantatas by Bach and Albinoni. I sat in the audience as the sun moved slowly down the stained-glass windows and the whole nave was caught in a prism. As the soloist lifted her head her voice hit the corners and alcoves, and in the sunbeams you could see dust fly and cobwebs vibrate. The musicians played selections from the *Brandenburg Concertos* and the audience sat there stiffly, all in evening dress, except for one sort who wore a T-shirt and wellingtons and had no one sitting next to him.

At the interval there were refreshments. A woman in a long purple dress came up to me and said: 'So what brings you to our lovely village?'

'I'm on the river. I've got a skiff. I'm travelling to the source.'

And she nodded her head and said: 'What star sign are you?'

'Star sign!? Er . . . Taurus.'

Then she shook her head and said: 'Oh no you're not,' and went back to her seat.

There was something cryptic about Dorchester. Afterwards, I walked through the village and it was if the place were under some sort of spell. A face with a long nose poked out of a hedge. A toby jug sat on a window sill and its eyes followed me as I walked past. There was a chill in the air and everyone had a grin.

And then the next morning when I climbed the Sinodun Hills, that rose above the trees on the opposite bank, I suspected that by coming to Dorchester I had walked through the looking glass. I crossed the river by the lock and climbed to a hilltop where some ancient earthworks lay smoothed by time, remnants of the earliest settlement on the Thames. The view was superb: ahead the river wriggled like a silver fish and the valley stretched away miles into the distance, while behind stood Didcot Power Station, a designated Site of Outstanding Natural Ugliness dominating the countryside the way only a power station knows how.

There was an adjacent peak topped with trees like a tuft of hair on a bald head. As I walked over to it I heard a lone voice singing sweetly. It grew louder the nearer I got to the trees but when I reached them it stopped and I found no one. It suddenly felt like winter. Boogie stuck his nose in the air and sniffed. I sniffed and smelt burning leaves. A man and a dog approached through the trees. He stopped and said: 'Was that you singing?'

'No.'

'Probably a transistor. They bring them up here at the weekend. My boy came up here for his birthday one year, at midnight. He's got some strange friends. I think one of them's a Druid. It's a nice spot though. Shame about the eyesore down there. Is that a Swedish bulldog?'

'Yes.'

'Thought so.'

I turned round to look at Boogie. From somewhere he'd got a french bread and honey-glazed ham open sandwich.

I didn't mean to spend long in Dorchester that day, but

I was distracted and ended up staying until the afternoon.
I lost a mooring iron and I was hunting round the bank
for it when a man passed in his dinghy and asked me the
problem. I explained my loss and he offered to give me a
stake he had. 'Let me pay you something for it,' I said. It
was only a bent bit of metal but it looked as though it
was an important part of his boat.

'Oh I couldn't take any money,' he said. 'You're in the
country now; folk help each other out. You'll do the same
for me one day.'

'Are you sure I can't give you something for it?' I said.

'Oh, okay then, give us ten quid and we'll call it quits.'

He asked me where I was going and when I said the
source, he said: 'Well, you're here.'

'Pardon?'

'Do you know anything about this Thames and Isis
business?'

'Not much.'

'Right, good. This is the start of the Thames here.'

I looked over the bank to where the Thames was visibly
continuing in a westerly direction and was about to protest
when he said: 'That's not the Thames, that river up there.
The Thames ends here. That's the Isis up there. And that's
the truth.'

I'd heard this story before: how, above Dorchester, the
Thames becomes the Isis. Other theories claim it becomes
the Isis as far back as Henley. Another theory claims it is
the Thames all the way to the source except for a brief
interlude in Oxford where it becomes the Isis. Then again,
others say it is the Isis in Oxford and Henley, but the
Thames above Oxford and below Henley and between
Moulsford Bridge and the third stile along past the caravan
site just downstream from the Beetle and Wedge.

But my friend had proof: 'Do you know anything about
the Romans and the Thames?'

'Not much . . .'

'Right, good. You see Thame is the old English word for river. So when the Romans arrived and asked the ancient Britons what the name of the river was they got the answer: 'It's called the river.' But the Romans couldn't cope with that. They liked giving rivers flowery names like the Tiber and so on, and so they decided to call the river the Isis after the Egyptian god. So it became known as Thame Isis, which in time became Thamesis and eventually Thames. And that's the truth.'

What he said was either a fascinating piece of etymology or absolute gibberish, but you can't say that to someone when they've just supplied you with a boat hook and so I nodded and said: 'I see. Listen, thanks for the boat hook. I've got to go.'

'Go where?'

'To the source of the . . .'

'I've just told you. You don't listen, do you?'

'Mmm.'

'So, you can come to the pub. I've got loads of interesting things about the Thames to tell you. My name's Jeff. Did you know, for instance, that Thames salmon frequently mistake Barn Elms Reservoirs for the North Sea?'

The pub had a beautiful garden with many people balancing veal and ham pie on their laps. I bought two pints of beer and some mackerel-flavoured crisps. Boogie had some cold tongue with piccalilli and a gherkin. Jeff spoke with his mouth full: 'Do you know anything about the Thames Barrier?'

'Not much . . .'

'Good, because in twenty years' time the thing will be useless. It's true. The polar icecaps are melting. By the turn of the century London will be underwater.'

'Who told you that?'

'Doesn't matter who told me. What matters is that the

Bank of England, Buckingham Palace, Wembley Stadium, the M25, all of them will be underwater.'

'Buckingham Palace underwater?' said an American voice behind me.

'You bet,' said Jeff, and introduced himself to the four American women sat at a table eating veal and ham pie. There was a great grandmother, a grandmother, a granddaughter and a great granddaughter. Boogie introduced himself as well, scoring off the great granddaughter, the granddaughter and the grandmother. The great grandmother though was harder to crack. She ate slowly and meticulously, never taking her eyes off her food. The grandmother said: 'She likes to eat.' Boogie gave his 'we've got something in common' expression, and moved in on her.

The women told me they had a hire car and were just driving. 'We've been to London, Bath, Stonehenge, York and Stafford,' said the great granddaughter.

'Why Stafford?' I asked.

'Because we thought it was Stratford,' said the granddaughter.

The pub closed. Everyone else had finished their meals a long time ago but the great grandmother still had a plate of blackcurrant and apple crumble and some cheese to go. Boogie was resting his head on her lap, giving her all his best faces, just waiting for her to look once into his eyes so as he could hook her, but she never looked away from her plate. He lay on the ground showing her his protruding ribs. Then he sat up and gave her his 'you could make me one really happy little dog, old lady' expression. But nothing. She spooned the food methodically to her mouth, scraped the bowl and sat back. Boogie hung his head in disbelief. I was shocked. The woman had had a three-course meal and Boogie didn't get so much as a crust. I'd never known him fail so badly. Fortunately, Jeff offered a reprieve. He said: 'Let's go for a walk along the towpath, and then go to the Abbey Tea Room. A real treat.'

'Did someone mention afternoon tea?' said great grandmother.

'She likes to eat,' said the granddaughter.

I wanted to get moving, but I couldn't deny Boogie this re-match, so I joined them all on a walk along the river. Boogie lagged behind. Like a gambler whose system has failed him he was frantically checking and rechecking his mathematics.

A swan came nuzzling up to us. 'If only we had some bread,' said the great granddaughter.

'I've got some bread,' said Jeff, and from his pocket he pulled out a packet of sandwiches.

'Oh, we can't take your sandwiches,' said the grandmother.

'Course you can,' said Jeff. 'You're in the country now. Everyone shares everything.'

'We must repay you somehow.'

'Oh, all right, give us a fiver and we'll call it quits.'

The sandwiches were fed to the swan who was partial to corned beef and tomato.

We found the Abbey Tea Room in the old cloisters that ran up the driveway to the abbey. Jeff led us to where the proprietress stood on the front step. He nodded to her and she completely ignored him. There was a Morris 1000 parked outside and I knew it was hers.

In keeping with the Dorchester allure there was an element of surrealism about the Abbey Tea Rooms. We were sat at a big round table in the middle of the room. On the wall a sign said: 'The taking of too much jam and butter will render the management violent.'

The proprietress spoke with assertion. She said: 'Your first time?'

'I've been here before,' said Jeff and she ignored him.

'If it's your first time I'd better explain. My ladies and I run this tea room to raise funds for the church. The system we operate is as follows: we supply the cakes and biscuits. You eat them and then tell us what you've had and we charge you a price slightly in excess of what it costs us to bake them, thus reaping a profit. It's a system that works quite well, we find.'

Then she turned and walked into the kitchen and immediately a troop of women bound in aprons descended upon us. They ran round with teapots saying: 'The first cup of tea is twenty pence, the next ten, the rest five.' Then they pointed their spouts of each of us in turn and said: 'Strong, weak or normal?'

Cakes, biscuits and scones were dispersed. At our table sat four generations of Americans all eating cake and shortbread and cream teas. Boogie positioned himself by the great grandmother. With cream tea at stake I knew his performance would be exceptional.

He began with basic clinical hypnotism. His pupils small, but rotating in opposite directions. This achieved no response whatsoever. Next he moved on to auto-suggestion – masticating, swallowing and licking his lips; he even belched for effect, but his opponent didn't blink. She finished her cake and licked her fingers and moved on to the shortbread. Boogie looked at me in despair.

The tea room filled up, but nothing was too much trouble for this noble collection of tea-ladies, they glided around the room as though they were on casters: 'Party of twenty-nine? Certainly, how many with milk and how many without?'

The great granddaughter said: 'England's just the way you expect it to be, isn't it?' And the granddaughter said: 'It's just like the films and the Agatha Christie books.'

'More cake anyone?' said a little lady in a cardigan with leather patches.

'Did someone mention more cake?' said the great grandmother.

'She likes to eat,' said the great granddaughter.

Boogie sat down by her again. This would be his last chance. But I didn't realize how desperate he'd become. As the great grandmother lifted a brandy snap to her mouth, Boogie nudged her chair. A cheap trick, but the brandy snap fell and Boogie opened his mouth in anticipation. Like a lizard the great grandmother flicked out a hand and caught the brandy snap, then dunked it in the cream and popped it in her mouth in one fluid movement. This was the knockout blow. Boogie started to watch the food rather than the face – a beginner's mistake. I knew he was in big trouble when he started to drool. Boogie never drools unless he's worried. The great grandmother ate the last piece of coffee cake and that was that. To rub it in she wiped her hands on him.

We all walked back to the boat, Boogie trailing, looking suicidal. 'Are you travelling alone?' said the granddaughter.

'A girlfriend's joining him in Oxford,' said Jeff.

As I climbed back into the boat the great grandmother gave me a paper napkin in which was wrapped a brandy snap stuffed with cream. She said: 'Give this to your little dog, will you? He looks fed up.'

They all stood on the bank and waved to me as I sculled away, and the granddaughter called out: 'We must meet for dinner when you get back.'

'Did someone mention dinner?' said the great grandmother.

'She likes to eat, doesn't she?' said Jeff.

I sculled away into the evening past a house where a bust of the Duke of Marlborough peeped over the hedge.

Then on through Clifton Hamden and under its pretty
bridge. As it grew dark I camped by what looked like an
abandoned swan's nest, made up of reeds and moss and
plastic bags, not to mention a car radio, a Lucozade bottle
and an old deckchair. I noted all this in my wildlife diary
under the swans' section.

The night was warm and I sat out on the old deckchair
– just me, the willows, the water and the breeze, and the
electrical glow, concrete, steam and wires of Didcot
Power Station that sat in the distance like a city. Inside the
tent Boogie lay severely depressed, confidence shattered,
racked with self-doubt. I said to him: 'Hey, don't worry,
champ, you've still got it. The woman was probably a
witch.' But he wouldn't be consoled.

Later, when I was eating my kedgeree with kippers –
Delia has a way with kippers – he glanced at me and I
pretended to be hypnotized by him, and spooned a great
dollop of rice in his bowl. This cheered him up margin-
ally, but I didn't give him the brandy snap, that would
have been cruel. It would also have been impossible since
I'd eaten it myself.

Power stations were to feature heavily the next day. I use
the plural because although on the map you will only see
one identified, there are at least five. They all look alike,
I agree, and people will argue that there is only one, but
if that's the case it moves around a lot. That morning
Didcot Power Station was round every bend in the river
and peeping through every hedge. I sculled away from it
and suddenly there it was behind me. I sculled towards it
and it sneaked up on my port side. It was confusing for
a while but then I realized that the river was hopelessly
lost and was doubling back on itself as it wandered about
trying to find Oxford.

And after a while I have to admit I grew a certain

affection for the power station. The sun beamed on its grey cooling towers, and the silver pylons that surrounded it were all embedded in fields of dazzling rape. It had a symmetry and a brilliance, and clearly the longer one lived with it, the more an integral part of one's life it became. The lock-keeper at Culham lock was a great fan. 'I love that power station,' he said. 'I dream about it. Sometimes on a nice Sunday I'll go and drive round it with the wife and our Peter and Lucy and we'll have a picnic by the perimeter fence.' I nodded sympathetically, and slowly rose to his level as ninety thousand gallons of water burrowed beneath me.

'I mean,' he went on, 'I'd much rather have that power station there than a scenic beauty spot. You know, an oak forest or an example of glacial drift, or a windmill or something poncey like that. Give me the hum and the glow of Didcot any day.'

He seemed like a sage, so I asked him if he had any ideas on where the source was, and he said:

'In Gloucestershire somewhere.'

'Could you be more specific?'

'Yes. It might be in Wiltshire.'

He went back into his cottage and I moved off. Then after I'd gone about a hundred yards he ran out again, waved his arms at me and shouted something. I hurriedly sculled back to him and he said: 'I almost forgot. You must call in at the Swan in Radcot. It's the best pub on the river.'

I made good time to Abingdon, a neat, double-yellow-lined, hanging-basketed town with friendly policemen. There was a great abbey here as long ago as the seventh century, but none of the original building remains. Instead there's a beautiful County Hall and around that there's a Halford's, a Dixon's, a Woolworth's and a Curry's, and a shopping precinct with ornamental tubs similar to the ones in Basingstoke, Exeter and Hull.

I spent my half hour in the town in Budgen. From the conversation in the queue I learnt that the one-way system was not what it should be, that the Nugent's boy was getting married (again), and that mature English cheddar was much cheaper in the market in Aylesbury. When I went in to the supermarket it was a peaceful spring day and I was cheerful. When I came out a gale was blowing and I was in a bad mood.

Litter blew down the medieval streets and fresh green leaves were ripped from their boughs and whistled hard down the river. Sculling was hopeless. It hadn't taken me long to get fit on this journey, just for my hands to get hard, but no amount of preparation could have equipped me for the battle with the wind. I'd be pulling away for all I was worth, and I'd look at the water and see the stream rushing past me, giving me the impression I was travelling at speed, then I'd look at the bank and realize I wasn't moving.

That evening, never in the history of sculling has there been so much mental effort devoted to the invention of a contraption that would enable a dog to row. I began to get frustrated, then angry. On the towpath a man with a poodle waved and said: 'It's all right for the dog, eh?' and I swore at him. 'Pardon?' he said. And I swore at him again.

Before long I made camp by the entrance to a backwater called the Swift Ditch. There's a theory that this was once the true course of the river, and that the monks at Abingdon diverted it to drive their mills. I took Boogie for a walk down the channel to see if I could find any trace of a navigation but it was all overgrown. I lost the path and emerged in a field where I sat in the shelter of a hedge until it grew dark, just watching a whole rape crop

sway in the wind. I was feeling chatty. I said to Boogie:
'I bought another packet of Winalot today. Five more
tokens. Only a hundred and fifteen more for the giant
wool-and-mixed-fibre blanket measuring sixty by one
twenty-five inches.'

Boogie sniffed a rabbit hole and gave me his 'what do
you want me to do jump up and down and do a cartwheel
and bark at the moon?' expression.

We walked on. An owl made a noise that resembled
the end of a factory shift. I said: 'So, Jennifer arrives
tomorrow. I bet that makes you feel happy. I mean, I'm
happy to an extent. Although I'm not really bothered one
way or the other. It would be nice to have her here, that's
for sure. But I'm not going to let it worry me.'

In the distance electricity cables were slung across the
land and the pylons strode towards Didcot.

Next morning I had breakfast with my shirt off sitting in
the sunshine on the quay at Sandford lock, and I decided
I'm at my best when I'm having breakfast with my shirt
off sitting in the sun on a quayside.

Then a large woman in sunglasses said with glee: 'It's
not going to last, you know. There's a low coming in.'

She said she lived in Oxford. She said she had a house
by Folly Bridge. She said if I saw people waving at me
from a red-brick house by Folly Bridge with a cheeseplant
in the window, it would be her and her grandchildren.

I said: 'I'll come in for a glass of champagne shall I? . . .
Ha.'

'No, I shouldn't do that,' she said.

Sandford had some pretty horses in its meadows and
some rotting, sinking barges on its riverside. These were
old college barges, the craft on which the Oxford colleges
would gather to watch their fraternity rowing teams in

action. Once they were lavish and exquisite queens of the river but now they were full of weeds and old newspapers.

But they were the first sign of what was to come – a stretch of the river dominated by the university, and, in particular, the university eights. I'd seen a few of these rowing teams in action before. One had flashed past me in the Pangbourne Reach, and then near Wallingford I remember being woken early one morning by a megaphone. There was a huge inhale and exhale of breath, a coordinated grunt and then a wave had hit *Maegan* harder than anything from a cruiser had ever managed. I whipped back the canvas and saw nothing but a ruffled river. But a few minutes later the thing returned. It resembled an animal more than anything. An octopod slicing through the surface like a glasscutter. The eight bodies balanced in the boat were glistening and steaming, all shoulders, and anything that got in their way wasn't struck so much as cut cleanly in two.

One boat I could cope with. I could cower in the willows till it passed. But above Iffley lock was something quite different. Here was a school of them waiting in the pound above the lock like sharks, blind with sharp edges. The crews were less impressive than the one at Wallingford, varying from gangling skinny youths to whom this activity was clearly compulsory, to squat chubby sorts stuffed into their seats, to whom the activity was also compulsory. They all had a freshman's innocence, but at the stern of each boat, wedged into position, sat the cox, and there was lodged the jaws of the vessel.

I watched for a while as the boats basked in the sunlight. Then I left them and set off upstream, imagining that they practised in that little corner of the river only. I did find it hard to imagine how they produced teams to win the Boat Race with that sort of training, but television is deceptive, and besides, I thought, if they used the whole river there'd be no room left for other craft like me, would there?

Suddenly there was a draw of water and a scream of sweat being forced through pores and round the bend it came, oars flapping in a fury, heading right for me, sharp end first. And from those little heads on the back of the boat came a string of abuse reserved traditionally for the rowers, but on this occasion redirected at me: 'Take the pressure, row, row, row, feel for the stroke . . . what the? . . . Get out of the bloody way! You! Yes you, you cretin! You with the ugly dog and the stupid hat. Clear off!'

I splashed wildly for the bank only to find myself in the path of another boat skimming along the water from the other direction, blades drawn. 'You're dead!' came a voice from somewhere and as the boat passed me I had the feeling I'd just been run through with a sword. Somehow I managed to weave a path as far as the boathouses and there I decided to wait until the rowers took their lunch break.

Inside the boathouses, the boats were carefully stacked. I snooped around, went up close to them and carefully touched one with my finger as if it might bite. Out of the water they'd lost none of their grace or their venom. They sparkled with gloss and varnish. They seemed as fragile as insects.

Above the boathouse were the grandstands that had taken over the role of the barges. A woman in a bright blue rowing shirt was sunbathing and drinking Pimms. She'd seen me moor *Maegan* and she laughed at Boogie and said: 'It's all right for the dog, isn't it?' which disappointed me, I'd have expected something more original from an Oxford undergraduate. She had a book open on her lap and I said: 'What are you studying?'

'Nothing,' she said. 'I'm a buyer for John Menzies. I'm a friend of Dave's. How about you?'

'I'm not studying anything either. I'm just passing through. I don't even know Dave.'

'Doesn't matter, no one here goes to the university. At least Mike, Clive and Tina don't. We just hang around.'

She explained the activity on the river. The boats were training for the Summer Eights, an important social and athletic occasion. The races were called Bumps because the river wasn't wide enough to enable the boats to race in line and so they competed a length behind each other, the aim being to bump the boat in front. A successful team ascended a position the following year.

We were interrupted by a commotion in the water up by Folly Bridge where the eights turned. A couple of drunk skinheads had hired a dinghy and were in the middle of the river behaving like pirates, trying to disrupt the college crews. The row boats came flying for them and the skinheads laughed and jumped up and down and then fell in the river. The eights' coaches, patrolling the towpath on bicycles, asked them politely if they'd mind behaving less obstructively, and the skinheads' response was to drop their trousers.

Oxford had its fair share of drunk skinheads on this balmy lunchtime. While the undergraduates were all rowing on the Thames or punting up the River Cherwell clutching strawberries and cream, behaving just as they were supposed to, the skinheads were outside the Head of the River with their shirts off, drinking Swan extra-strong lager, behaving just as they were supposed to. One big egg-headed lad was standing on the balustrade of Folly Bridge shouting to his mates: 'Watch this, watch this!' then he'd leap in the river with all his clothes on and climb out giggling, and repeat the stunt. It was harmless and mildly entertaining until *Maid Unexpected* appeared from

upstream heading for the bridge. The skinhead, oblivious
to the approach of the boat, climbed up on the bridge and
prepared to launch himself once more. His mates could
envisage just what I could – *Maid Unexpected* emerging
from under the bridge to twelve stones of closely shaven
and vividly tattooed youth smashing through her roof.
This isn't the sort of thing you see every day and I was
tempted to stand by and watch the performance, so indeed
were his mates who were suddenly paying far more attention than they had before. Fortunately, someone warned
him just in time and *Maid Unexpected* motored under the
bridge with the occupants sitting at the dining table eating
salads. They smiled and waved at the skinheads who
responded with the bare bum treatment again.

I had some time before I met Jennifer but I'd planned
it this way because I wanted to visit Merton College, one
of the earliest Oxford colleges, dating from 1264, and a
fine example of the Decorative and Perpendicular period.
The fourteenth-century library had a rare collection of old
books and manuscripts and it was these I particularly
wanted to see.

But it was shut, so I bought some strawberries off a
couple of undergraduates pedalling a strawberry and
cream wagon about town and then lay down in Christchurch Meadows until two o'clock when I was standing
outside Boots as prearranged. By three Jennifer hadn't
shown and the staff in Boots were giving me funny
looks. I closed my eyes when I heard the familiar roar of
a powerful motorbike from round the corner, hoping it
would pass by, but it stopped of course, and Michael the
motorcycle messenger strode towards me.

'Hello.'

'Hello.'

'Me again.'

'Yes.'

He handed me the familiar carrier bag, 'Indonesian today. Satay with peanut sauce and coconut pieces.' I took the bag and put it straight in a bin marked Keep Oxford Tidy. Michael then gave me an envelope. I tore it open; it read: 'Call me as soon as you get this. I've got bad news.'

I screwed it up and threw that in the bin as well. Michael said: 'You're angry now, aren't you?'

'Yes, I am.'

'I think that's good. Now you've got to show her you're angry. It's all very well coping with it but if you really care for her, you'll risk everything and express your anger directly. Anger is a positive emotion. You must always remember that.'

'Oh fuck off!'

I found a phone box and called her. Her PA answered.

'Hello, it's me. I want to speak to Jennifer Conway, now!' Boogie started barking. Passers-by peered at me through the broken glass of the kiosk.

'She's not here,' said the PA with an unfamiliar urgency. 'But I'll give you a number where you can reach her.'

I dialled the new number. I'd be angry with her all right. I'd tell her to forget it. I'd announce that Boogie was here. I'd say: 'Boogie's here, and he's good company . . . well, he's not bad company . . . well at least he's here.'

Jennifer came on the line. She said: 'Mark, I'm so glad you've called. Thank you for worrying about me. I suppose you thought something had happened to me. Well it has. I'm in hospital. I've had a car accident. I was on my way, I really was.'

'What!?'

'Nothing serious. They want to keep me in for a couple of days for observation. The firm have insisted. I smashed the car up. I've bought another one though. Another TVR. A blue one. I hope you're not angry.'

'No, no, of course not.'

'I mean I suppose I could discharge myself but . . .'

'No you mustn't. You must stay there. This is terrible.'

'It wasn't my fault even. A taxi driver hit me on Putney Bridge. He'd just got his licence back, he said. Did you get the satay?'

'Yes. Thank you. Listen are you sure you're all right?'

'Yes. I'll be with you on Thursday, promise. I can't wait. I've got my bag with me now, all packed. I'll come straight from hospital. What's that barking? I can hear barking again.'

'I'm calling you from outside a pet shop. Oops, my phone card is running out. See you Thursday.'

I stayed in Oxford a while and peered in at some undergraduates sitting in big rooms swotting, but the city was choked with traffic, and the heat was getting to everyone. I felt I should stay longer and look round, but I felt happier out of urban areas. I also felt happier on the river and it seemed to ignore Oxford once it passed Folly Bridge. In most towns the Thames attracted parklands and salubrious housing and was a desired area. But in Oxford, after the splendour of Christchurch Meadows, it took on the appeal of a canal and snaked through the back yard of the city past terraces, under railway bridges and round the back of factories and allotments.

'Not putting your spinach in now are you?' said a voice from behind a hedge.

'Course I'm putting my spinach in now,' said another.

'Too early.'

'I always plant my spinach two days after the full moon in May.'

'Rot!'

That was the sort of talk I wanted to hear, and I gave an extra tug on the sculls.

The only other event to mark my exit from the city was an episode at Osney Bridge. As I emerged there was no empty yoghurt tub in the back of the boat, no newspaper, no drink container and no fresh fruit cores, instead there was a ten-year-old lad, dripping wet.

And suddenly I was under attack as a group of his mates swung from the trees on ropes and splashed into the water round *Maegan* and tried to clamber over her gunwales. Boogie sat up at this point which caused the pirates to stop and reconsider. One said: 'What sort of dog is that?' and I replied: 'he's a doberman alsatian, and he's in a bad mood so I should clear off.'

Boogie's problem is that he doesn't quite have what it takes to be a ferocious guard dog. His natural disposition is to smile at intruders and say: 'Hi there! C'mon in.' He's about as aggressive as a welcome mat. His only weapon is his tongue, although on this occasion that did the trick. As the kids started to grab my sculls and anything else they could lay their hands on, Boogie leant over the boat and licked the leader.

'Eagh, he licked me. He licked me,' screamed the kid. 'I'll get Aids.' And that did it.

Osney Bridge was low, just how low I didn't realize until the other side where I saw a sign proclaiming 7'6". This prohibited many cruisers from continuing upstream and one could sense the river beginning to enter another new phase. Past the entrance to the Oxford Canal the land flattened and stretched. On one bank was a shady blaze of sycamore and hawthorn, while on the other, water meadows stretched for miles, and horses, cattle, swans and geese all stood together in the heat haze, drinking at the water's edge.

Gone now were the No Mooring signs. No longer were

the spires of the towns and villages and the metallic flash of motor cars drawn to the water. The river was suddenly wilder and more exposed. I put my hat on for the sun and set off for Gloucestershire. A grebe swam across my path and disappeared into a clump of weeds. There were a few thumps, some gasps and some squeals and a moment later a couple of bruised ducks, a limping magpie and a Canada goose with most of its feathers missing crawled out.

8. See You on Tadpole Bridge. And That's a Promise

Tadpole Bridge was just twenty-five miles upstream from Oxford but it took me three days to reach there. The pace of the journey changed, so did my lifestyle. I emerged as a waterman with crusty hands and a dirty neck. I began to degenerate. *Maegan* began to look messy. Only the blossom that tumbled from the hawthorn and chestnut trees kept her fresh. She looked as though Boogie and I had just got married in her.

The breeze was with me for a change and I sat easily in the saddle of the boat. I lost the sensation of travelling. I was just following a rail and had no control over my destination. The rain came as everyone had predicted and so I travelled with the tent half unfurled to form a canopy. It acted as a sail and I was blown westwards. Then whenever a shower came I'd roll down the sides and be watertight in minutes. I'd sit there wrapped up out of the damp as the warm rain made the river steam, and I'd watch the dragonflies land on the water and disappear into the pink gob of a chub.

I liked to watch the rain. It felt reassuring to see the land drink it up. It was like a transfusion, and there was a reverence about the whole process. There was a silence just before the first drop and then the reflections would begin to disintegrate as the river surface grew agitated. The grey cloud merged with the grey water. The songbirds were quiet, and Boogie would sit on the end of the boat with his mouth open.

I'd never realized how noisy rain is in the country. The leaves cracked and the grass shivered, and the meadows and woods were dented as the rain and wind pelted them. The showers were never long but they were a display and everything stopped until they were over. And then there was a sense of celebration. The river sparkled anew. Cuckoos, pigeons and magpies poked their heads out from trees. There was an irresistible smell of wet grass. The ducks came out and started squabbling. The gnats gathered in clouds and did whatever gnats like to do. The pylons began to hiss. A train shuddered in the distance over wet rails. Somewhere upstream a lorry splashed through the puddles over a five-hundred-year-old bridge. The cracks in the mud were filled. The river was a millimetre higher, the grass a shade greener, the earth watered. And then there'd be a blue crack in the sky and shafts of sunlight that made my hat steam. The reflections returned as bright as before and I'd look around and make a note of how well I had got to know cow parsley on this trip.

After almost two weeks on the water I was easily pleased and my days were gloriously indulgent affairs. Boogie too seemed settled. He was aware of the change in our surroundings in so far as he was totally confused now whereas he'd been only moderately so before. I remember him one afternoon standing on the bow, ears pricked, a daisy chain around his neck, sniffing the air in that intense way he does, giving the impression he is sorting out every smell and every sound and identifying them as only an animal of instinct can, whereas the truth is he hasn't got a clue what any of them are. As soon as we lost the diesel smells of Oxford he was baffled.

And now the wildlife became more prolific and less shy. I got to know the water rat population well. I saw my first curlew – a humorous creature if ever there was one. And I watched the herons for hours. One landed very close to me one evening and I watched it fish as darkness fell. It stood motionless, staring into the murk, and then every so often its head would dart into the stream and emerge with a grin all over its face and a struggling silver fish in its beak. The bird would swallow visibly and then resume its stern posture.

If I wanted supplies I'd walk to a village. They all had little supermarkets, and all the little supermarkets had little queues. But for some reason these no longer bothered me. In one I turned to the woman behind me and said: 'Would you like to go in front of me since you've only got three items?' And she eyed me suspiciously, but edged her way slowly to the front, then paid her bill and ran out.

My only other link with humanity was the lock-keepers. They were my source of information and I relied on them. At Eynsham the keeper was planting his annuals for the coming bank holiday weekend. He said: 'It's much quieter on the river now. You should have seen it twenty years ago. It was busy then but I liked it. I liked it when you had to collect money and there were really long queues.' And he recalled how before boats were licensed each vessel had to pay a toll to pass through the lock. 'Your skiff would have cost ninepence,' he said.

I told him I was looking for the source and asked him if he had any knowledge on the matter and he said: 'All things considered, if you were to ask me that question what with me being a lock-keeper and having a working knowledge of the river, particularly so above Oxford, I'd have to say I don't know a thing about it. My! will you

look at the size of that?!' A perch had come to the surface.
I knew it was a perch because the lock-keeper said: 'That's
about the biggest perch I've ever seen. Fifteen years ago,
before they cleaned the river up, they had all but
disappeared.'

The weir streams were less frantic now, and the locks
smaller and all manual. In place of hydraulics the keepers
had long poles and big muscles. They were mostly local
people and their lifestyle more reclusive. At Shifford lock
I even managed to have a look inside a keeper's cottage.
He came flying out when he saw me approach and began
to wind up his gates for all he was worth. He said: 'You're
not trying to break any records are you? 'Cos if you are
I've got bad news. One of my sluice gates is stuck.'

I'd heard stories of teams of rowers heading downstream as fast as they could trying to break records, but
the very idea seemed appalling. Over the last few days I'd
become convinced of what I'd always suspected to be true,
the Thames can be anything you want except a rush. So
I said to the lock-keeper: 'Yes, I'm trying to break the
record for the slowest time between London and Lechlade.
I've taken nearly two weeks so far, what are my chances?'

'Pretty good, I'd say.'

I asked him if he had a toilet I could use, and he said I
could use his own. I regarded this as a privilege and
thanked him graciously, then walked up his path to the
house imagining rooms full of flowers and river memor-
abilia, a boiler, a tiled fireplace, the smell of soup and
smoked willow. But it was a dump. It wasn't even lived
in. The only furniture was a microwave and a table with
a half-completed Airfix kit scattered around it.

I pulled *Maegan* up the river, keeping a steady rhythm,
taking time to think about what I saw. How, for example,
did that pair of checked trousers end up in that hawthorn
bush? It was a mystery probably very few people could

explain. Placenames began to interest me as well. We'd passed Moulsford, Oxford and Swinford, and I'd satisfied myself they were all places where it was possible to herd mules, ox and swine across the river. This theory rather faltered though when we reached Duxford.

I was also confused by the bunkers on the river's north bank. I asked the lock-keeper at Pinkhill what their history was, and the answer, although straightforward, was interesting because it illustrated what a barrier the Thames has always been, from the time when man first began to walk the Ridgeway, through the Roman and the Norman occupations, right up to the Second World War. It was during that war, when the threat of a German invasion was real, that the Thames was designated the line of defence behind which the country would retreat should the Channel coast be taken. Provision was made to blast every bridge over the river, and bunkers were built every mile. The lock-keeper said: 'Bunker's a good name for them, I reckon. That's all they're used for now – bunk ups. Huhuh.'

In the evening I'd find a pub if one was near, or I'd pull the canvas over and sit in the lamplight, and try to write poetry. These were unproductive evenings though. I only ever wrote one poem and that was to Delia Smith. She was beginning to play an intrinsic role in the expedition, far more intrinsic than Boogie, anyway. He spent his evenings lying in the bottom of the boat, dreaming, making strange noises as he re-enacted the television programmes he was missing.

He and I were becoming better company though. I remember on the Tuesday night I camped in a wild spot. I don't know the name, I just remember there wasn't a house or road or light to be seen, just the distant pylons. We'll call it Dogford because Boogie, in an effort to get a drink of water, dived into the river, or rather he leant over the side of the boat too far and fell in. Why he should even have attempted this I don't know since his water bowl was always full of fresh water and sat wedged in the bottom of the boat. And yet ever since his first taste of river water he'd regarded it as vintage and would drink no other.

I pulled him out, saving his life for the fourth time. We sat on the grass. Boogie looked at me and gave me his 'stupid dog eh? falling in the river' look. It occurred to me that the river had cast its spell over him as well, and might be helping him to find the inner animal. Later when we went for a walk along the towpath, I whistled tunelessly and said: 'The thing is, see, Boogie, the thing we've got to understand is that if someone's behaviour seems unreasonable the chances are it's indicative of something more deeply rooted. Just as the real reason Jennifer has kept me waiting for two weeks is locked away within her, your tendency to fall in the river is probably a result of your traumatic upbringing and being orphaned at an early age and suffering the ignominy of being beaten up by cats all the time. You could be a depressed dog, but don't worry, I know a very good vet.'

Boogie licked something horrible off a stile and we walked back to the boat.

I was just about to crawl inside the tent when I could see a figure in the fading light about a half mile away. It was a man striding across the field towards us. I watched as he approached, his hat at an angle, his baggy trousers bulging at the pockets. He walked straight up to me and invaded the space one doesn't normally invade when you're meeting someone for the first time, particularly if it's in a lonely field at dusk. I thought he might be about to ask me back to his house for champagne but he looked at me from eye to eye and said: 'Evening!'

'Evening.'

'One pound fifty, please.'

'What?'

'One pound fifty.'

'What is?'

'The cost.'

'Cost of what?'

'You camping on my property. It costs one pound fifty.'

'What?'

'You're camping. This is a farm camp site. I'm the farmer. It's simple enough. One pound fifty.'

I looked behind me. I looked in the distance. I looked to either side. There was nothing but fields and woods and mist I said: 'This is a camp site?'

'That's right.'

'You're joking.'

But he wasn't joking.

I thought: Okay, if he wants to be like that, and I said: 'But I'm not actually on your property am I? I'm on the water.'

'You're on my bank. Your mooring irons are on my bank. It's seventy-five pence a mooring iron. If you had an anchor it would be all right, but you haven't so that's one pound fifty.

The pylons hissed. An owl made a noise like Roy Orbison. This was about the quietest, least spoilt spot I'd seen on the river, and this man must have walked miles to charge me for standing on it. I said: 'If this is a camp site where are the toilets and the showers and the camp shop selling Camping Gaz refills, and where's the ping pong room?'

'Three miles away in the village. It's a big camp site.'

I was having such a pleasant evening until he arrived. I paid him to get rid of him and said: 'What's your VAT number then?'

'Same as yours. Goodnight.' And as he walked off into the mist he called out: 'If you're going to Lechlade try the Swan. Best pub on the river. My nephew works there.'

Back in the tent I undressed and grumbled and searched for my sleeping bag. 'All right, Boogie! I'm in no mood for games. Get off it!' But he wasn't on it. I looked everywhere a sleeping bag could sensibly have got to: in the luggage, under the seats, in the lockers. Then I looked in silly places where a sleeping bag could never have got to: in the Winalot bag, in the bilges. But the thing had disappeared.

Then I looked outside. It was a beautiful, misty blue night. The moon on the wane. The water the colour of a Milk of Magnesia bottle and very still. The only clue that there was a current at all was the cylindrical silhouette of my sleeping bag floating slowly back towards London.

There are many ways a dog can show his loyalty to a human being but there can be none more altruistic than sharing his blanket in a time of crisis. And Boogie took no persuading at all that night, I'm proud to say. All I had to do was inform him of the soaking wet sleeping bag situation, and that my sleeping bag falling overboard was in effect similar to his blanket falling overboard since we were a travelling team, and that I wouldn't hesitate in letting him share my sleeping bag if the needs were reversed, and he understood completely. I gave him the decision, of course. I told him it was up to him. He had every right to say: 'Get lost! Get your own blanket.' But his response was typical. He did shriek as I whipped the blanket from under him, and then bared his teeth and made primitive wolf-like noises, and his eyes turned red, but I knew this was merely a playful performance to try to draw maximum humour out of the situation, to keep spirits up.

And apart from the occasional strange smell and him

grinding his teeth in his sleep, it was a perfectly comfortable night. I dreamt that Jennifer was lying next to me. Her shoulders were bare just above the blanket. I was attracted to the smooth curve between her collar bone and upper arm. I put my hand out to touch her. She looked beautiful but she had a cold nose.

Then I was woken by birdsong. It was eight o'clock, I felt a touch of dejection. I'd travelled up a hundred miles of river and I still hadn't got up in time to see the sunrise. What sort of explorer is it that never gets up before eight o'clock? I asked myself, and I steeled myself for a swim. I lifted up the tent flap and saw the water laced with a thin cold mist. The idea of immersing myself battled with the idea of going back to sleep and to Jennifer. I turned over, and there, staring at me, was Boogie. He licked me and grinned. I know I don't look my best in the morning but I don't look anywhere near as bad as he does.

The river continued to narrow. The willows hung their boughs in the water. I began to see faces in the gnarled trunks, grotesque faces. In some places the trees had been blown over in the storms of the previous winter and now they lay on the land, the bank beneath them pulled up like a curled lip. I didn't see many people during those days. The river was secretive now and it crept up on villages. It may only have been a half mile from a main road but it had become a master of disguise, lurking beneath its banks and willows like a nervous animal.

But the few people I did meet were sympathetic characters who seemed in touch with the spirit of the river. One afternoon I saw a woman walking along the bank. She called out: 'I never thought I'd ever see one of those again, not this far up.'

She was referring to *Maegan* and so I paddled over to her. 'We used to have a skiff like that when I was a child,'

she said. 'My father would row us up from Oxford to
our bungalow. That was in the twenties. I've not been in
a boat for years now.'

I asked her if she wanted a ride upstream and her eyes
lit up like a child's. She must have been seventy years old
but she jumped in the back seat and said: 'It's all right for
the dog, isn't it?'

She was a farmer. She and her husband had retired and
bought some land near Northmoor but they weren't doing
well. 'We keep cows but as soon as you reach your quota
that's it. It's not enough to live on. We should move into
sheep; there's money in sheep.'

A magpie flew overhead and made a noise like an owl.
'Noisy buggers magpies,' she said. Then she lay back and
used Boogie as a pillow and said: 'It's so nice to be back
on the river again. We had a boat once but a pig trod on
it.' A B52 flew overhead and the river shook. 'Noisy
buggers, B52s,' she said. 'Can I have a row?'

She climbed in beside me and we sculled up to Bablock
Hythe. There had been a ferry across the river here for
almost a thousand years, but it had recently ceased oper-
ation. The woman said: 'No one looked after it. Not even
the Thames people. They didn't take an interest and it got
too bad to repair.' The same thing seemed to have happened to the pub. The Ferry Inn it was called and it had
weeds in the car park and smashed windows. 'The landlord didn't pay his electricity bill and they cut him off.
He should have looked after that ferry. But the river's
changed now. The motorboats have changed everything.
They've driven all the wildlife away. You don't see any
kingfishers any more. Sorry, I've dropped a spoon of
yours overboard.'

We pottered about the river up to Northmoor where
she climbed out. I told her I was heading to the source

and asked her if she knew anything about it and she said: 'No. But Kelvin will.'

'Kelvin?'

'You'll find him in the Dun Cow in Northmoor. You'll like the Dun Cow. It's full of life. All the youngsters go into the Dun Cow.'

I moored by Northmoor lock and that evening walked the two miles to the Dun Cow. Northmoor seemed to be the most remote village I'd come across, but arriving in villages on a footpath from the river gave me a different perspective from arriving by car. I normally surfaced through the back yard of a village, through the churchyard or a housing estate, rather than in the traditional way on a road, over roundabouts and past a Welcome To sign. The locals always looked surprised to see a stranger appear in their midst in this way. I felt like an alien and since I didn't have a map with me all I knew of my location was that it was somewhere west of Oxford.

Many eyes watched me as I walked through Northmoor. I could see movement behind net curtains. I went into the Dun Cow leaving Boogie lying down outside in front of a pot of geraniums. I was the only person in the pub. Presently one of the many doors opened and a woman came out tying up her apron: 'Always quiet on a Wednesday,' she said. The room was a sitting room with armchairs and pot plants, prints and books, and no bar, just a doorway with barrels. I was pulled a drink and told to make myself at home.

The barmaid sat down with me as if I'd just walked into her house and needed to be entertained. I asked if the animal in the field by the side of the pub was a donkey and she said: 'It's a hinney.'

'A hinney?'

'A hinney.'

'What's a hinney?'

'A cross between a stallion and a female ass. You're not from round here are you?'

'No.'

'You've got a boat on the river haven't you?'

'Yes.'

'A rowing boat?'

'Yes.'

'Rowed from London haven't you?'

'Yes.'

'Thought so. I go to London sometimes. The Tower. Hampton Court. Vince Hill's house. I don't like it much.'

'I'm looking for the source of the river. I want to speak to Kelvin.'

'He'll be in later.'

A couple of elderly regulars came in and sat down. 'Put my spinach in today, I did,' said one.

'Too early,' said the other.

'Too early be buggered.'

'Too early. Don't put spinach in till third weekend of May,' and he laughed and put his head back to show off his hairy nostrils.

'Ha, you'll be laughing when you've no greens.'

'You have to have greens,' said the barmaid. 'A meal's not a meal without greens.'

'Too early for spinach.'

I chipped in with my newly acquired knowledge on the subject: 'It's best to plant spinach two days after the full moon in May, I've always said.'

'He's waiting for Kelvin,' said the barmaid.

Everyone looked out of the window. They seemed like people who had come to the pub every single night for the last forty years, and yet they could still amaze each other with a conversation about rhubarb. But, it was more than just a conversation. It was a celebratory recounting of the day. They sat in silence now but silence was a very important part of the process. And I was so obviously the stranger because the silence made me fidget. I felt responsible, I could hear the clock tick. I smiled a few times; smacked my lips a few times. Then looked round the room, pretending I was fascinated by a picture or an ornament.

The eldest man brought out a coach timetable and flicked through it. 'Taking my girlfriend on an outing, I am,' he said.

'She won't go with you,' said his mate.

'She will. I'll make her.'

'Where're you going anyway?'

'Romsey. They've a good brewery there.'

'I used to go to Romsey to buy cattle.'

'Don't see so many cattle about now. I was just thinking tonight as I walked here and saw the empty field. You don't see many cattle like you used to.'

I bit my lip then said: 'There's more money in sheep, isn't there?'

'Kelvin will be here soon,' said the barmaid.

Everyone looked out of the window again. There was another silence. A car pulled up.

'There's Dave,' said the barmaid.

'That's never Dave. Since when has Dave had a green car?'

'It's his sister's.'

'It's his mum's,' said the barmaid.

Dave came and sat down. He said: 'Whose dog is that?'

'Mine,' I said.

Everyone in the pub looked out of the window at Boogie. He was eating a leg of chicken with rice and pepper salad and garnish. I said: 'He's getting old. But they get old, don't they, dogs?'

'He's waiting for Kelvin,' said the barmaid.

'Kelvin's on holiday on the Algarve,' said Dave.

'Oh yes,' said the barmaid. 'Kelvin's gone on holiday to the Algarve. I forgot.'

'Yes, he's gone to the Algarve,' said the other two.

I walked back to *Maegan* across the fields and under the pylons. A handful of swallows darted in and out of the wires. We reached the towpath and walked back towards the sound of the weir stream. It would take time to become a local in Northmoor, I decided.

I said to Boogie: 'I've been thinking. It might be an idea to live together when we get back.'

He licked some cuckoo spit off a thistle.

'Not you. I don't mean live with you. I do live with you. Unfortunately. I mean live with Jennifer. I feel as though I've somehow got to know her better on this trip. Even though she's not arrived yet. How would you fancy living with Jennifer?'

Boogie looked up at me, he had a dead fish in his mouth.

Back in the boat I lay down surrounded by the sound of the weir stream but it was as murmurous as a lullaby now.

Then it was Thursday afternoon and I was on a telephone at Tadpole Bridge speaking to Jennifer's PA.

'Is Jennifer Conway there?' I said.

'Is that you?'

'Yes.'

'Well, she says she's coming this afternoon, although I don't believe it myself.'

'I'd like to speak to her please.'

'Yes, yes.'

The Muzak was *Chariots of Fire*. Jennifer came on: 'Where are you?'

'Tadpole Bridge.'

'I'm on my way. I'm coming tonight. I can't wait.'

'. . .'

'Hello?'

'You're joking?'

'No, I'm not joking. Meet me on the bridge at six.'

'You're really coming?'

'Yes.'

'. . .'

'Hello?'

'There's something I've got to tell you.'

'What?'

'There's something you should know . . .'

'Yes?'

'I've been meaning to tell you this for some time . . . I've got . . . I've got a shortage of spoons, can you bring some?'

'Spoons?'

'Yes.'

'Right.'

There was a pub by the bridge. I went to the gents' and looked at my reflection. I was filthy, knotted and hairy. I looked at Boogie. He was filthy knotted and horrible. I walked back to *Maegan*. She was filthy and littered, full of willow and hawthorn, duck feathers, crisp packets, soft drink containers, sweet wrappers, colour magazines and apple cores all lobbed at me from countless bridges.

First I turned to *Maegan*. I swept her out, scrubbed her gunwales, coiled her ropes, tidied her cabinets and aired her canvas top. Then I turned to myself. I stepped into the shallow river, shaved in my reflection, dried out my sleeping bag, washed my clothes, and laid them out over the canvas. I combed my hair back, scrubbed my nails, and put talcum powder into my wellingtons. Lastly I turned to Boogie. After which I had to turn back to myself and the boat again. On the dot of six o'clock I was sitting on the handsome parapet of Tadpole Bridge wearing

damp underwear. Boogie was at my side sitting to attention, hair parted, not a scrap of muck on him. How could
anyone resist him?

The first hour passed quite quickly and pleasantly.
When the sun set it cast a magnificent one-eyed reflection
of the bridge on the water downstream. The second hour
passed more slowly and was more boring. I counted the
radio masts in the fields to the north and I squinted at the
military aircraft just a few thousand feet up. Presently a
local character with slippers on his feet sat down next to
me and told me his name was Ivor.

'That your dog?' he asked.

'Yes.'

'Messy, isn't he? What sort?'

'Nicaraguan dachshund.'

'Thought so.'

Before he could change the subject a car had stopped
and a woman wound down her window and said: 'Can
you tell me where Bampton is?'

Ivor stroked his chin, looked both ways and said: 'Two
miles that way, turn left and it's on your right. This is a
Nicaraguan dachshund, by the way.'

The woman looked at Boogie and smiled and said: 'I
once had a dachshund. It was called Roman. We bought
it off a family who were going to have it put down because
its leg was damaged at birth. But we nursed it and looked
after it and it grew healthy and was a marvellous pet for
years, wonderful with the children. It even won prizes.
Then it squeezed under the garden fence one day and ran
across the road and a car hit it.'

We sat in silence. I could hear rooks down by the river.
The woman looked very sad. Ivor said: 'What sort of car?'

She drove away. I said to Ivor: 'Waiting for the pub to
open?'

'No. I don't go in there. It's got a stuffed fish on the

wall. I often come and sit on the bridge, though. I direct the traffic. I live in Bampton.'

Another car pulled up. The driver wound down the window and said: 'Is Hinton Waldrist round here?'

'Two miles that way, turn left and it's on your right,' said Ivor.

The car drove off. Ivor said: 'They need directing, see. People in cars are always lost. They depend on people like me.'

We sat there in silence. I was getting to understand the timing of these silences now though, growing more comfortable with them. As Ivor mused I imagined Jennifer and me lying in separate sleeping bags at either end of the boat. Then I imagined us in a double sleeping bag in the centre of the boat. Then I imagined Boogie lodged in between us. Ivor said: 'I've been sitting on this bridge looking at the river for years.'

'I bet you've seen it change?'

'Everyone asks me that. He's ugly, your dog, isn't he?'

The woman who had stopped earlier drove past and stopped again. I asked her if she'd found Bampton. She said she had, eventually, and added: 'When I was a young woman I walked up from Oxford to Lechlade along the river towpath. I remember there was a wonderful village square at Bampton; tonight I was just passing and wondered if it would be how I remembered. I seem to recall having my sandwiches under a big tree and a woman came up and gave me a bag of raspberries and I ate them all the way to Lechlade. I imagined the square would be much smaller than I remembered, but strangely it was bigger.'

There was a silence. The woman looked sad once more. The rooks were quietening down as the light faded. A low-flying aircraft roared overhead polluting the moment. When peace returned Ivor said: 'What sort of sandwiches?'

The woman smiled and said: 'Can you tell me how I can get back on the Oxford road?' And Ivor stood up and said: 'Two miles that way, turn left and it's on your right.'

I waited two hours exactly and then went into the pub. It was called the Trout. Boogie had a half gammon steak, some grilled tomatoes, and some creme caramel, then he came and sat down under the table. I patted him. 'I'm through with that woman,' I said.

Boogie belched.

'If she turned up now I'd tell her to go home again.'

There were a few people at the bar. I made comments about the stuffed fish on the wall, about the beautiful reflection of the bridge in the water at sunset and about the assortment of military aircraft in the sky. This earned little response, so then I asked the barmaid how she cut her finger. She looked at me and said: 'It's always quiet on a Thursday. Only gets busy when we get a nice day, and we never seem to have those on a Thursday. Is your dog hungry?'

'No, he's not.'

I sat down. People were looking at me strangely. I wanted to get back to my boat and get sculling. A stool squeaked on the stone floor. A man with his shirt outside his pants turned to me to speak but before he could say anything a blaze of light hit the pub as outside four head-lights spun through the car park. There was the crunch of tyres that cost £97 each on the gravel. A car door slammed.

'Hello,' said a man looking out of the window, 'a TVR,' and into the Trout walked Jennifer.

Behind her came Ivor.

Ivor was the first to speak. He said: 'This young lady has asked me out for a drink.'

Jennifer stood there in a green jump suit and baseball cap. She looked at me hard for a moment, and took in my new waterman's appearance. Then I strode towards her and kissed her and I remember the rim of her hat dug into my forehead. The local characters watched silently with drinks poised. One man had hiccoughs. Jennifer took her hat off and I expected to see her hair fall. But she'd had it cut, cut short. At first I didn't like it then very quickly I decided it looked lovely. She said: 'I'm here.'

I said: 'Yes.'

She said: 'I'm late but I'm here. I've got luggage. Where's the boat? It's a beautiful night. I've got luggage.' And I think she may have been about to kiss me again when there was a shuffle below the table and Boogie struggled out from under a chair. He had a baked potato skin in his mouth. Jennifer looked at him. Boogie looked at her. Her face fell. So did his. Her body stiffened. His tail went between his legs. She said: 'What's he doing here!?'

I panicked and said: 'I don't know . . . he must have followed me.' But she didn't see the funny side of that remark, so I said: 'Listen: whilst you were in Paris, Oslo and Bologna, Boogie has been my faithful companion for a hundred miles of river and . . .'

'Well, introduce me to your friends,' she said, but she was already introducing herself. 'That's a fine fish,' she said, indicating the stuffed job in the glass case.

'Chub,' said the local character with his shirt hanging out of his trousers. 'Interesting fish the chubb, shy, likes cover, tricky to coax out. Got to be up early to get a chub.'

'Do you want a drink?' said Jennifer to Ivor.

'If you insist I'll have three pints of bitter, please.'

Jennifer moved to the bar. She said to the landlady: 'Is it always this quiet on a Thursday?' And the landlady said: 'It livens up later.'

We all played darts. We all bought rounds. As the night

progressed the pub filled and we all made friends. Ivor
followed Jennifer around all night. The chub fisherman
offered to take her fishing if she'd like to meet him on the
bridge at five thirty. It was the best night of the trip so
far. Then I said to her: 'Are you hungry?'

'Starving!'

We walked back to the boat along the towpath. Boogie
lagged behind. We carried armfuls of luggage. She'd
brought her tennis racket. She'd brought bathroom scales.
She'd brought six pairs of shoes. She'd brought the col-
lected works of W. B. Yeats, Wilfred Owen and John
Donne. She'd brought spoons.

'You've brought spoons,' I said, excitedly. 'Great.
Spoons.'

She looked at me and smirked and said: 'Have you been
all right on your own?'

'Yes. Of course. Fine. I've had a great time. Boogie has
been a good friend and . . .' As I spoke I could have sworn
I heard a telephone ring.

'Can you hear a telephone ringing very close to us?' I
said, but she was already digging into her bag. 'It'll be
for me,' she said and produced a white Vodaphone. I
looked on aghast as she composed herself for a moment
– ran her fingers through where her hair used to be –
and then answered the instrument: 'Jennifer Conway . . .
Why? . . . Why? . . . No . . . Why? . . . No.' Then she
put the phone away, smiled and walked on.

As we approached *Maegan* I could see a cruiser had
moored next to her. A big fat chrome-and-Formica job
with a lifeboat and a deep freeze. It was named *How's your
Father*. It dwarfed *Maegan*, made her look like a broken
branch off a tree. Sharp lights pierced the blinds and I
could see the flicker of a TV.

Jennifer said: 'Oh she's splendid. She's magnificent.

She's everything I ever thought she'd be. She's even got a lifeboat.'

'Er . . . No, this is *Maegan* over here,' I said, pulling back the damp moth-eaten flap.

Jennifer is used to not showing her emotions. That's why she's such a good businesswoman. That's why she's good at poker. That's why touching her you often get an electric shock.

She said: 'She's splendid! She's magnificent. She's everything I ever thought she'd be.'

I climbed in and lit the lamp. Jennifer followed and immediately the boat was full. Boogie decided to sit outside. I fed him his daily tin but he hardly touched it.

'I'm going to cook you fried mozzarella with a Provencale sauce,' I said and I took out Delia Smith. 'This is Delia Smith.'

Jennifer looked askance and said: 'Are you sure you've been all right while I've been away?'

'I've been fine. I've had lots of adventures,' and as I added the garlic, chopped tomatoes and basil to the onion and pepper I told her about the wild supermarket of Weybridge, the mad dog of Hennerton Backwater and the deadly rowing eights in Oxford. She sat there entranced, and then as I sliced the mozzarella in quarter-inch strips and coated them with seasoned flour, then dipped them in the egg mixture, Jennifer told me about Paris, Oslo, Bologna and Lisbon and her lunch date with Tiny Rowland.

'Lisbon?! I didn't know you went to Lisbon!'

'Just for the day. Waste of time. I did write a poem though: "Cabo di Roca I'm standing on your tip, like a rocking stone I'm trapped, with just a tumble or a trip, what voyage of discovery I would map . . ." It's awful, isn't it?'

'It needs just a touch more basil, and it's ready.'

We toasted each other with a bottle of claret and she said: 'I'm glad I'm here at last. I've always wanted to come away with you.'

And I said: 'I always knew you'd come.' From outside the boat came the sound of a dog being sick.

The meal was a disaster. It tasted strange. We struggled to eat it. The most memorable moment of the meal came when Jennifer dropped a mouthful from her fork on to her lap. She went to pick it up but there was suddenly a black flash as Boogie dived into the boat and grabbed it. Jennifer, playfully, went for him with her fork, but I held her back and explained that Boogie considered anything fallen on the floor as his. She protested. She said it had landed on her lap. I explained that since she was sitting on the floor Boogie had been confused. She said in that case Boogie had better watch his Kennomeat from now on because if he dropped any she'd have it in a sandwich out of spite. I told her not to worry: Boogie had never in his entire life dropped a morsel of food.

But this didn't spoil the evening. Jennifer quickly calmed down and we talked about the journey. She asked me if I'd visited Oscar Wilde's cell in Reading Gaol. I admitted I hadn't. She asked if I'd visited Mapledurham House where Alexander Pope was inspired, not to mention Galsworthy. I told her no. She asked me if I'd visited the meadows between Eynsham and Godstow of which Matthew Arnold wrote: 'Through the Wytham flats, Red loosestrife and blond meadow-sweet among, And darting swallows, and light water gnats, We track'd the shy Thames shore.' And I said I must have passed it but I couldn't exactly remember that bit.

I suggested instead we discuss the expedition. I said: 'The information I have is all rather based on hearsay but it appears a large piece of water does leave the main river just after Cricklade. Some call it the Swill Brook, some the River Churn. We'll find barbed wire across the river and we might have to carry the boat a couple of miles, but I've heard there's a tree . . .' And then Jennifer started to yawn. She said: 'I want to go to bed. Where does the dog sleep?'

'In the boat, of course.'

'What! Doesn't he sleep outside?'

'Boogie is my constant companion. He's been at my side throughout this journey. He's a member of the crew.'

'You've been watching too many Lassie films. He's a dog. He'd probably prefer to sleep outside.'

'We'll let him make the decision,' I said and took Boogie for a walk along the towpath.

It was a longer walk than usual. The moon was a marble. I could see veins running through its face. A chub plopped. Boogie stopped, sat down and scratched his ear more aggressively than I've ever seen him do before.

'She's a character, you've got to admit that. It'll take her a while to settle into the river's routine, of course. But don't worry about her. We're a good team, Jennifer and me. We work well together. Anyone can see that. It's good to have a woman on board as well, isn't it?

We walked on. The water slapped against the bank. My wellingtons glistened in the moonlight. 'It's a lovely night. The sort of night to sleep outside under the stars, to really get back to nature. I would do myself but I've got company. I don't know why you don't, though? You being a dog and all that. I mean it's your decision of course. You can sleep where you want. But I just thought it might be nice for you to sleep outside.'

Boogie stopped and banged his head on a gatepost. I thought it was an accident but then he did it a second time. When we got back to *Maegan* I paused on the bank and patted him: 'Listen, Boogie, I wouldn't normally ask

you to do this. But . . . it's our first night together. You
don't want to play gooseberry, do you?'

I pulled back the flap and he dived in and ran over the
pile of dishes and bedclothes to the stern where he lay
down and started to snore.

'He's made his decision. He wants to sleep in the boat,'
I said.

Jennifer was lying in her sleeping bag. She had a vest
on and the gas light made her shoulders flare as they had
in my dream.

I went through my going-to-bed routine. I placed all
the breakables in the stern, all the foodstuffs at the bow.
I put the milk outside to keep cool. I arranged the kettle
and the stove for the morning so I could just lean out of
bed and turn it all on. And I made sure my torch, matches
and notebook were handy. Then I brushed my teeth and
watched the white trail of Signal drift down towards
Oxford. I was so excited I dropped my toothbrush over
the side. 'The river has a gentle, soothing effect,' I said.
'It wraps itself around you. I've never felt so calm as I
have the last two weeks. I feel as though I'm having little
say in where the boat is taking me. I'm just following a
groove that I've no control over. The river has, I think,
more than anything else, made me feel insignificant. It's
made me . . .'

'Are you going to sleep with me tonight?' said Jennifer.
She was leaning on her elbow and the light illuminated
the little black hairs on her forearms.

'Yes,' I said.

'Good.' she said, and then she zipped the sleeping bags
together.

Later that night an owl hooted at last.

9. What? Lechlade Already?

Jennifer and Boogie have never got on, not since the time they first met and Boogie made a mess in her handbag.

They're such uncompromising characters. Boogie dismisses Jennifer the way he does pedigree dogs. He thinks she's pompous, discriminatory, opportunist, whereas none of this is true. I've tried to communicate to him that Jennifer is simply a perfectionist. She likes things to be without blemish. Boogie's problem is he isn't satisfied with something unless it's covered with blemishes. The more blemishes the better is Boogie's motto. That night on the boat was the first time they'd seen each other for years, but it hadn't been long enough as far as Boogie was concerned. He was outraged at the idea of Jennifer joining the expedition. Over the last two weeks he'd established certain parts of *Maegan* as his territory, and now it had been invaded. He felt usurped.

The next morning I woke early. Light was streaming in through the canvas. At the end of the boat Boogie lay with his eyes open, but next to me was an empty space. I looked at my watch: it was seven o'clock and something was splashing about in the river. Then two hands grabbed the side of the boat and there was Jennifer.

'I suppose you've been for a swim every morning?' she said. She took her wet T-shirt off and threw it into the boat. It landed on top of Boogie who leapt up as if some-

one had plugged him into the mains. Jennifer laughed.
Boogie shook himself and covered her with wet hairs.

It was a lovely day. 'Breakfast?' I said.

'In a little while,' she replied, and then she put on her
running shoes and set off along the towpath. She ran for
four miles she said, then, when she came back, Boogie
and I lay in the sun surrounded by buttercups and watched
as she did aerobics for twenty minutes. Then she dived in
the river again. When she finally climbed out, she said: 'I
suppose you do that every day as well.' I shrugged and
scratched my hat. Boogie licked his bits and went back
to sleep.

For breakfast we had croissants, figs and yoghurt,
orange juice and herbal tea. Jennifer breathed in deeply
and said: 'You're the only person I know who would take
me to somewhere like this.' Then she went back to the
car and returned with more luggage. She was well
equipped for the trip, there was no doubt about that. To
her already sizable pile she added a guitar, a wok and a
selection of pot plants. 'I couldn't trust anyone to water
them for me,' she explained, securing a philodendron to
the bows.

So I explained that that was the very reason I had
brought Boogie along, and she turned sharply and said
that she hoped that me bringing Boogie wasn't deliberate
after she'd expressly asked me not to. She said she hoped
she couldn't sense a power struggle. I said that a power
struggle was exactly what I had no choice in sensing,
considering her behaviour and the amount of time she'd
kept me waiting. She said if she'd known Boogie was
here I'd have been waiting a lot longer and that it seemed
ridiculous that a grown man couldn't go anywhere without his stupid dog. I said how thoughtless she was and
that if she respected me she should respect my dog as
well. And then she said who said anything about respect?

I was only a travelling companion. I backed off here and said that if we went on like this any more we'd have an argument. She suggested we were already having an argument and if we needed one to clear the air then we should have one. It was at that precise moment that Boogie, who had wandered off at the start of this altercation, came charging back to the boat hotly pursued by a herd of Jerseys. He jumped into the middle of breakfast with his dung-covered feet while the cattle screeched to a halt on the bank. Then the ones at the back started pushing the ones at the front going: 'Go on! Get in there and get the little bugger, you saw what he did to Margaret,' until one of the front rank lost her footing and her two front legs landed in the boat. Staring into the face of a cow I did what I considered to be the most noble thing – I clapped my hands loudly and threw a croissant at it. Jennifer, who clearly wanted to release some aggression anyway, hit the creature over the head with her wok. It was then I remembered my plan was not to react to her but to be reasonable, and so when the cow had got out of the boat I said: 'Anyway, the whole business doesn't really bother me'. And I think she may have been about to raise the wok to me when the phone rang.

She ran her fingers through her hair, composed herself momentarily as before and then spoke into the instrument: 'Jennifer Conway . . . Why? . . . Why? . . . No . . . No.' Then she put the phone away carefully and looked at me so as I could see the whites of her teeth. I decided it was time I took charge.

'Time we were heading out,' I said as authoritatively as I could. 'We've got some sculling to get done,' and I went to untie the moorings. But I'd tied a half-hitch sheepshank with a bowline reef the previous evening and the dramatic effect I'd hoped for was lost while I spent the next twenty minutes unravelling the tangle.

★

The problem with two people sculling together is that they have to keep in time. A missed beat results initially in much crunching of sculls and ultimately in a trail of zig-zags. Jennifer, who was in the stroke position, was powered by aggression and from the pace she was setting she clearly had a lot of it to work off. I looked at the bow wave we were creating and estimated our speed at about 20 knots. Having just got the coots to trust me I was now sending tidal waves to terrorize them.

We passed Rushey lock, where the beautiful garden was made even more colourful by two peacocks. The lock-keeper said: 'I used to have more, but they don't get on with the plants.' He leant on his shovel and smiled at us, time on his hands. 'You know something,' he went on. 'You're the only people I've had through here this morning.' And Jennifer said: 'Well get a bloody move on then. We're in a hurry.'

'Right,' said the lock-keeper, taken aback. As we rose up he saw Boogie and said: 'It's all right for the dog, isn't it?' and Jennifer said: 'Just open the gates, will you?'

'Right,' said the lock-keeper and he wound up the sluice gates as fast as he could. As we paddled out he said: 'If you're going up to Lechlade call in at the Swan, it's the best . . .'

'Where's your toilet?' said Jennifer.

'We haven't got one,' said the lock-keeper. 'We've got a wastepaper bin but no toilet.'

'You must have a toilet. Where do you go?'

'I've got my own. It's an unofficial one.'

'Where is it? Or I'll go on your petunias.'

'Er . . . First door on the left down the hall.'

Jennifer leapt out of the boat. I turned to the lock-keeper and said: 'Sorry. Her first day on the river.'

'Most of them are like her,' said the lock-keeper. 'My problem is I bottle it up.'

'Mmm.'

We licked up the river through meadowland, and flashed under Radcot Bridge, the oldest on the upper river. Someone threw a piece of orange peel at us but it fell in the water behind the boat. We were too fast for it.

The wind picked up. But half the time it was a headwind and half the time a tailwind, so erratic was the river's course. Jennifer said: 'Why does the river meander so?' And I replied: 'It's a very simple and natural process following inescapable laws of physics. If a river finds an obstruction in its path, say, sediment or a tributary stream or even fallen debris, the river course diverts. The deflected current hits the opposite bank where it carves the land away, and the underflow carries the resulting sediment, depositing it on the inner curve. As the surface current ricochets back to the other bank another meander is created, and the process is repeated until the river becomes a series of curves, changing the shape of the flood plain constantly. The longer it runs the bigger the curves become, thus in the case of the Thames, by the time it reaches Essex, the meanders are miles apart.'

Jennifer stopped sculling and my oars crashed into hers. She turned round and said: 'Who told you that?'

'A lock-keeper.'

Then she tensed and said: 'Quick, hand me a piece of paper; you've inspired me.' I tore a piece out of my notebook and handed it to her and she was silent for a while as she wrote in snatches. Then she punctured the paper with a full stop and said: 'Thank you, you made me write that. I knew this trip would be like this. It's wonderful. You must have written lots of stuff. Poetry is so therapeutic. Listen. About this morning. I'm sorry about our disagreement.'

'So am I.'

'I'm glad I'm here.'

'So am I.'

'Want to hear my poem?'

'Sure.'

'It's not finished yet. But the ideas are there. It's about reflections and how you forget they're there and then suddenly you see them again and realize they're always there. Everything on the river happens twice.'

'That's my idea.'

'What do you mean?'

'I noticed that almost as soon as I started on the trip.'

'So what?'

'Well, nothing, I was just pointing out that I was struck by all the reflections as well. I wrote it down myself. About how the reflections give the river its extra dimension, how it's easy to forget about them and not notice them for long periods, but then suddenly you can see the whole earth and sky in the water.'

'So you're saying I've stolen your idea?'

'No . . . I'm just . . . let's hear it.'

'No, I don't want to read it to you now.'

'Go on.'

'No.' And she leant into the sculls again.

In the afternoon we reached Kelmscott. I felt tired. I lay on the grass while Jennifer went for a jog to 'warm down'. When she came back she said: 'William Morris used to live in Kelmscott. I'd like to go round his house.'

William Morris's house is a beautiful sixteenth-century Cotswold stone manor house that just peeks over the trees to catch the river. Morris moved here from London to escape the pressures of his public life but he made the mistake of leasing the property with a fellow artist, Dante Gabriel Rossetti, who shared Morris's life rather more than Morris would have wished, falling in love with Morris's wife, Jane. Rossetti painted her again and again, in a way you wouldn't normally paint the wife of the man you've just leased a house with. Morris, depressed by the whole business – although unable it seems to do much about it – buried himself in his work, producing unrivalled designs for ceramics and fabrics, many of which are still kept at Kelmscott House. The house is open to the public only a handful of days during the year. Fortunately the day we were there was one of them.

We left Boogie guarding the boat and walked out of the heat into the cool, panelled house. It was a treasure of tapestries and furniture. We looked at each other and knew we were in a precious place.

A small number of people were quietly walking around, speaking in whispers. The couple in front were gazing at a tapestry. The woman said: 'It's just like Eileen's, only more complicated.'

I put my arm through Jennifer's and we controlled our laughter. I said: 'Shall we get a place like this?'

'You're not serious?'

And I wasn't but she looked at me in a way that made me think she'd be disappointed if I was joking. So I said: 'Yes.'

Then she looked disappointed so I said: 'Well . . .'

'You and me, live together?'

'We get on okay.'

'No we don't.'

'We do.'

'We argue all the time.'

'We don't.'

A woman was showing the visitors round. We were attracting attention. I stopped beneath a tapestry and put my arm through Jennifer's again. She said: 'No one has ever wanted to live with me. I'm selfish. I'm a loner. I use people.'

'No, that's just the image you give. I know it's a veneer.'

'No it isn't.'

'It is.'

'Listen, I'm telling you it isn't.'

'C'mon. It must be.'

A man with dark glasses was looking at us. He turned his head away but I knew his eyes were still focused on us.

'Besides,' said Jennifer. 'I couldn't live with that dog.'

We walked through the village. It was the most beautiful I'd seen on the river. There was a stone fence around a meadow. There were dovecots in walls, pigs in back yards, vegetables in the gardens and Volvos in driveways. The spring had laundered everything in inimitable fashion. The foliage was unblemished and unravaged. The blossom on the chestnut trees was a perm fresh from the salon. Nothing was fat, flaccid or pale; all was small tight and vivid, and I remember that day in particular for the irresistible sense of optimism to be felt when the first warm spell of the year arrives and you know that summer is finally here, and the best part is it's all still to come.

Eventually we found ourselves in the churchyard standing over Morris's grave. ' "Love is enough; though the world be a-waning, And the woods have no voice but the voice of complaining." He was a refreshing poet,' said Jennifer.

'It would really please me if you'd just try to get on with Boogie.'

'I will on one condition.'

'What's that.'

'He doesn't moult, breathe, or fart in my direction ever again.'

'Listen, he's not as unpleasant as all that. He's not a puppy; he's an adult now, responsible and mature. Treat him with respect and he'll repay you in the only currency he has: loyalty.'

Jennifer sighed and smiled and we walked back to the boat. As we crossed the field to the river Boogie was lying in the stern snapping at a dragonfly and Jennifer said: 'All right. What does he like to eat best of all?'

'Curry,' I replied.

'Tonight we shall have curry. Where's the nearest takeaway?'

'Probably in Oxford.'

'I'll call Michael my motorcyclist to . . .'

'No! Delia and I can make a curry.' And although we were still a hundred yards from the boat, as soon as that wonderful word was uttered, I saw Boogie sit bolt upright on the back seat and look around wearing his 'okay, who said curry?' expression.

Outside, the day lay dying. The water meadows of Oxfordshire slipped into a mist. The sun went down behind the electricity lines and melted. On Radcot Bridge a great crested grebe knocked an old-age pensioner off his bicycle. *Maegan* sat very still on the water.

Inside, we were wrapped in the thick and heady aroma of a Sri Lankan egg curry. I sat at one end with Delia Smith in one hand, a wooden spoon in the other. Jennifer sat opposite, chopping up onions. Boogie sat behind her, his eyes full of tears.

As I added the garlic and ginger to the chopped vegetables, I told Jennifer of my desire to be a lock-keeper. As I blended in the turmeric, flour and curry powder just as Delia instructed, and stirred it to soak up the juice, I said: 'We could get a lock-keeper's cottage – something like the one at Sonning. I could be the lock-keeper and you could be the lock-keeper's wife.'

'I want to be the lock-keeper, you can be the lock-keeper's wife.'

'I don't think there are any female lock-keepers.'

'Well, we'll soon see about that, won't we?'

As I mixed in the creamed coconut and added a tiny bit of lemon juice to sharpen the flavour and then poured the sauce over the eggs and rice and chutney, Jennifer asked me how much lock-keepers earned. I told her I imagined about eight thousand pounds a year but that included electricity and the house came rent free. She told me she'd earned eight thousand pounds in the time I'd been on the river.

The curry tasted dreadful. It was a disaster. Boogie loved it but that meant nothing. We ate what we could then piled the rest into his bowl and he ate it the way he always eats curry – quickly. Afterwards, I washed the plates in the river and watched the orange slick drift off towards London. Then Jennifer said: 'It's Friday. I want a night out on the town.'

We walked up the lane to the village pub, arm in arm, Boogie at our side. 'See, he's cute once you get used to him,' I said. Jennifer patted him and something brown came off on her hand.

'It's only curry,' I said, but I wasn't sure.

The pub was empty but for a few men sitting round the bar. The landlord said: 'It's always quiet on a Friday.' Jennifer ordered the drinks. She said: 'Pint of bitter and . . .' She was interrupted by one of the wits at the bar. He said: 'And what's your fella having, a Slimline tonic?' He laughed and all his mates laughed with him. I cringed. Jennifer calmly continued: '. . . And another pint of bitter and a Castella.' Then she lit the cigar and swigged back half a pint, and said: 'Okay, who wants a game of arm wrestling?'

The men weren't local. They came from Yorkshire. They were itinerant barn erectors. They travelled the country putting up barns wherever they were asked. 'We even went to France to put one up once,' said a lad with shaving cuts on his face. 'Have you ever been to France? Great place, France.'

I remember him because he was the first to take up Jennifer's challenge.

'Arm wrestling with a woman?' he said. 'Don't be daft.'

'For a fiver,' said Jennifer.

'I wouldn't take your money,' said the lad.

'A tenner,' said Jennifer.

'I wouldn't rob you.'

His mates were gibing him. 'Fifty quid,' said Jennifer. There was a hush. 'Put your money away,' said the lad, feeling uneasy now.

Jennifer leant over him and said: 'Beat me and you can sleep with me.'

His mates yelled and pushed him off his seat.

'Er . . . okay,' said the lad, and blushed.

They sat at a table in the middle of the room. The lad put fifty quid on the table. They held hands; their grips tightened. The lad's hand hit the table so hard it caused the ashtray to leap on to the floor.

'Next,' said Jennifer and a big lad from Featherstone got up and sat at the table. He put his fifty quid down in front of him and said: 'Can I sleep with you as well?'

'Sure,' said Jennifer, and she nearly broke his wrist.

The next challenger was a man in a T-shirt with the word Rams on the back. He said: 'I once built a barn on the Glasgow Ring Road all on my own.'

He sat down and fixed his upper lip into a snarl. Then he grabbed Jennifer's hand, and for a moment it seemed as though she had a match. But she was only playing with him. Suddenly she lunged, bringing his arm down to the wood with such force he nearly fell off his stool.

She pocketed a hundred and fifty pounds, then walked back to the bar and ordered another round and said: 'Anyone else fancy a go?'

'I'll have a go,' I said.

'Okay sucker,' she said and we sat down at the table. I took her hand and she let it go limp and I slapped it down.

'You win,' she said. 'Your place or mine?'

'Mine.'

'Let's go.'

We walked back through the village, laughing. The night was so bright it was blue. Jennifer's shorn hair sparkled. I felt very close to her at that moment. I was about to tell her so when the phone rang.

She stood there in the icy grey reflection of the Kelmscott stone. She breathed in heavily and exhaled slowly, then she picked up the receiver. 'Jennifer Conway . . . No!' Then she replaced it in her bag again and we walked back to the boat through a field of cows.

Maegan looked more of a home now she had two people living in her and pot plants dispersed around her deck. But as we climbed inside and settled down, an appalling smell threaded itself through her. The air had taken on a different consistency and I knew instantly that Boogie had farted horribly.

Jennifer looked at Boogie and grimaced. I said: 'That's not Boogie. It's the cows. I'll go and frighten them off.'

I took Boogie for a walk along the towpath, a longer walk than usual.

'Now look! I know what you're trying to do. You're trying to antagonize her, aren't you? You're trying to show what disgusting company I keep. Well let me give you a word of advice: she's trying to get on with you. And I think the least you can do is try and do the same. Now, I know you've just had a curry, and I know what an impressive farter you are, and I know you're merely exercising your right to fart, but I'm warning you – you are living on a knife edge, boy. One more word out of your bum tonight and you are going home Red Star.'

When we got back to the boat Jennifer was in the sleeping bag. I ordered Boogie to the stern and crawled in beside her. She said: 'Do you really think my aggressive image is just a veneer? Do you think that beneath this selfish and cynical exterior there's a woman you could live with?'

'Yes.'

'I don't.'

'You're not trying.'

'It's always the same. The people I like don't stay around me long and the people I dislike stay around even less. I've a self-destructive streak in me. Anyone who gets close to me I hurt. It's because of what happened as a child.'

I had a feeling I was about to hear something she told very few people. I remember thinking to myself: The river has got to her already. I said: 'Yes?'

'I've never told this to anyone . . . My mother deserted me shortly after I was born. I was left on a doorstep. The nurses called me Jennifer after the policewoman who found me. I was brought up in a variety of foster homes around the Docklands. Once, when I was six, I was locked in a darkened bedroom for three days. I've always had to look after myself. And now it's instinctive for me to think of no one but myself. I'm full of resentment.'

The water lapped on the mahogany. Outside an owl made a noise like a washing machine. I suddenly realized how alike Boogie and Jennifer were. I felt elated. I said: 'Of course! You're just like Boogie. He was . . .'

'What!!' And she was up and out of the bag and staring at me with tears in her eyes. 'I've just told you the most private thing I can, and you say I'm like your dog. You're sick . . .'

'No, the point I was trying to make was that I'm used to the problem of . . .'

'You're weird. I've heard you talking to that animal as well. I don't know what you've been up to on this trip but it doesn't seem very healthy to me. I don't know how much more of this I can stand.'

'No, listen to me . . .'

'I don't listen to people. That's the first thing all the people I know, know about me. I'm unreasonable.'

'We can work on it. I'm just the opposite. I'm incredibly reasonable.'

But she'd turned away.

I lay there feeling the chill in the air. I felt helpless. I leant over to touch her but as I did so I plunged my head into a cloud so vile it made my nose run. At the back of the tent I could see Boogie's eyes green with mischief, his teeth starry in a grin.

'Not now, Boogie, please. This is a very insensitive time to fart,' I whispered.

Jennifer stirred and sniffed. 'What's going on? What on earth is that smell? It can't be . . . Oh my God! Get that dog out of here. Get him out!!'

I thought quickly: 'Er . . . actually, that was me.'

'What?'

'That was me. I did that. I'm responsible for that rather distasteful smell. Sorry.'

In the half light I could see a look of disbelief on her face. She shook her head and settled down again. I glared at Boogie. He glared back and lifted his rump and trumped again. The canvas around us sagged.

'You'll pay for this, you will. I promise you, you will pay for this.'

Like a marsh slick, the fetid cloud slipped from beneath him and drifted towards me. I furiously wafted my hand at it but it was too powerful. Jennifer stirred again. She looked at me, her face creased in pain. 'That can't be you?'

'Yep. Sorry. That was me again. The curry, I'm afraid. Huh.'

At the back of the tent Boogie released another. It curled its way towards us. 'Oh no!' said Jennifer as she inhaled the fresh blast. 'That's the most foul . . .'

'Sorry. Me again,' and I tried to grin. 'These little idio-syncrasies are what you learn to get used to when you live with someone. You know, the Real Me, and all that.'

'If that's the real you, you can sleep on your own!' she said, then climbed out of the boat and went and slept under a willow.

The river was becoming more shallow. In the past few days we'd passed the confluences of sizable rivers like the Evenlode and the Windrush and their contribution to the stream was missed. I began to grow concerned about the water level. If it was this low here what would it be like past Lechlade? Jennifer's arrival had distracted me and I felt it was time we re-established our commitment to the river. I decided we should hold an expedition meeting.

I was roused the next morning by a flash of light as the tent was ripped off the boat and there stood Jennifer pant-ing and dripping. She'd been for another run and swim. She had little white socks on that just covered her ankles. She threw her arms out and said: 'Happy birthday!' and then she dived on top of me and kissed me like a vacuum cleaner. 'How did you know it was my birthday?' I asked.

'I never forget birthdays. C'mon, breakfast is ready. Today is your day. I'm doing all the cooking.'

We had scrambled eggs and crispy bacon with garlic mushrooms, followed by pancakes and maple syrup and espresso coffee. The day was dazzling and the ducks flew in and gathered round the boat. The sun shone on their beaks and we threw them some wholemeal toast. Jennifer seemed to have put the events of the previous evening to one side, although I noticed that when she cut the rind off her bacon she threw it to the ducks rather than to Boogie. He went for a walk along the towpath at this point.

After breakfast Jennifer pulled a box out of her bag and presented it to me. 'Many happy returns,' she said. I unwrapped the box carefully and folded the paper. It was a pair of binoculars and from that moment on the journey was never the same.

I focused on the ducks and immediately they took to the air and disappeared. I focused on a family of coots and they flapped and panicked and splashed into the safety of the reeds. I saw a rookery in the distance and the moment I focused on it the birds ducked down into their nests and became quiet. I saw a swan upstream but when it realized I had my lens trained on it it up-ended and showed me its tail. It was as if nature could tolerate only a certain amount of intrusion by man. Casual appreciation was encouraged, but binoculars were voyeurism and that wasn't allowed.

But I didn't tell Jennifer. I told her instead I was thrilled with my binoculars. I told her what a thoughtful, kind person she was, that she couldn't have given me a nicer present and that I was so glad she was here with me to see all this. She said there was nowhere she'd rather be, that she spent too much time in the city and not enough in the country, and that she needed to have people like me around her instead of the sycophants she worked with. She needed to change her priorities, redirect her energies in more spiritually rewarding areas, and she should begin by properly involving herself in this trip, and if the phone were to go now she wouldn't even answer it.

At that point the phone rang. Jennifer tensed then answered it. 'Jennifer Conway . . . Why . . . Of course . . . No . . . I don't care.'

She put the phone back in her bag. 'Sorry,' she said.

'It takes time to acclimatize, that's all,' I replied. 'It takes time to slow down into the rhythm of the river. You'll see. I've been wanting to say I think we should concentrate our efforts now on getting to the source. We should put all our petty differences behind us and remember we have a goal.'

She nodded and picked up her orange juice and stood up in the boat: 'To the source,' she toasted.

'To the source,' I replied, and we packed up and sculled away with the sun in our faces. A bark from the bank reminded me I'd forgotten Boogie.

At Buscot lock, Jennifer said to the lock-keeper: 'We're heading to the source of the river, any advice?'

'Yes, my advice is you'll kill yourself at the Castle Eaton Rapids. If you do get to though to Cricklade though, there's a pub you should call in at but I forget the name.'

'The Swan?' I said.

'No, there's no Swan in Cricklade.'

This was the first sign that Cricklade was a place beyond the limit of navigation. The lock-keeper said: 'It's different up there. Wild and, well . . . different.'

Then past the lock the spire of St Laurence's of Lechlade came into the view for the first time. I stopped sculling and ran to the bow, and stood on the end of the boat with my hands in the air: 'Lechlade. I can see Lechlade!' I said.

'What? Already?' said Jennifer.

'What do you mean, already? This is the beacon I've been heading for ever since I left London.'

'What's so special about Lechlade?'

I told her that Lechlade was the end of the navigable Thames; how from here on it was everyone for themselves; how the Thames Water Authority didn't advise any boats to venture further; how cruisers would run aground within a mile or two.

I tried to impress upon her the significance of the first sight of the spire of St Laurence, how the sight of it filled me with a spiritual warmth that only a traveller who has journeyed under his own steam could appreciate. I also tried to impress upon her how from here on the comforts of the downstream river would be denied us. Ahead lay the period of privation that must be endured in any search for the source of a great river, and that from now on things would get tough.

And she said: 'Great. Let's have lunch. Spaghetti with a Mexican sauce, I think.'

We moored under a willow. Jennifer dug out her hat. It was squashed and chewed and largely ruined. She sighed and said: 'That dog has slept on my hat. Look at it!'

'I'm sure it was an accident.'

'It's my new hat. He's squashed it.'

'Its green; it looks like grass. You're lucky he only slept on it.'

'I'm a tolerant person but there's . . .'

'You're not tolerant. You're intolerant. You're confusing the two.'

She screwed her face up which made her look painfully attractive, then she sat on the bank with Delia Smith in one hand and a clove of garlic in the other. A heron flew past and landed on a bough nearby. I picked up my binoculars and focused on it, and it flew away to hide in some trees.

As Jennifer cooked the chopped pepper and added the garlic she said: 'There are dog hairs in the olive oil.'

I said: 'I feel as though I've formed a special relationship with willows on this voyage.'

As she added the minced beef, red wine, chilli powder and parsley she said: 'There are dog hairs in the tomato puree.'

I said: 'Willows are such mournful trees. I feel their

arms reaching out to me. Weeping is the only way to describe willows.'

As she brought a pot of salted water to the boil and fed in the spaghetti, she said: 'There are dog hairs in the boiling water.'

And I said: 'I see faces in their bark; devilish faces.'

She started to grate some Parmesan cheese but then stopped and said through clenched teeth: 'There are even dog hairs wrapped around the cheese grater.'

'I'd like to be buried under a willow.'

'Did you hear me? There are dog hairs wrapped around the cheese grater.'

'Yes . . . they're mine.'

She held one up. 'Your hairs are not black and curly.'

'Ah, that could be one of Boogie's.'

'Of course it's one of Boogie's; they're all Boogie's. The dog is falling to bits.'

'Yes, it's a problem. Dog hairs in your bed, dog hairs in your bath, dog hairs in your soup. You'd be surprised how quickly you get used to it.'

'I don't want to get used to it. I don't feel as though I should have to get used to it. It needn't be like this, you know.'

'What do you mean?'

'Well . . . it's unkind to have a dog in the city.' She served out the spaghetti. It smelt strange. 'It's unkind to have him on the boat.'

I looked over at Boogie. He was looking very suspicious.

'We could find a nice home for him,' went on Jennifer

She put some Mexican sauce on my plate. It looked like mud.

'Have you ever thought about having him fostered?'

'Yes . . . No! He's my companion. He's my sidekick. How can you say such a thing? How can you be so cruel and thoughtless? That dog has come through thick and thin with me. He's . . . why has my Mexican spaghetti got hairs in it?'

In the afternoon we sculled towards Lechlade at speed. We had aggression to release again. At one point we overtook a cruiser called *Bridget's Legs* and Jennifer shouted at it to get out of the way. The driver shouted back: 'Look, it's *Three Men in a Boat*,' to which Jennifer stood up and retorted: 'I've three points to make here: 1) I am not a man 2) *Three Men in a Boat* is, in my opinion, a self-indulgent, blinkered book and nothing but English sentimentalism at its worst, not to mention being flagrantly sexist and I resent being in any way connected with it. And 3) I think your boat stinks.'

The driver of the *Bridget's Legs* reddened. I said to Jennifer: 'How could you say that?'

'His boat does stink.'

'About *Three Men in a Boat*?'

'Oh, not you as well!'

We passed through St John's lock, the highest on the river, where the statue of Father Thames reclines in front of the lock-keeper's house like a centrefold. Then at four o'clock in the afternoon, *Maegan* slipped under Lechlade's Halfpenny Bridge. A young girl waved and shouted. I waved and shouted back and she threw an empty milk carton into the boat, Jennifer caught it and threw it back and hit the girl on the nose.

We moored and I tied a double clover bowline with a reef on the second loop and a granny spring. 'We're here,' I said and put my arms out in a reconciliatory fashion.

Jennifer smirked and hugged me and said: 'Right, into town; we need provisions.'

'What for?'

'Your birthday party of course.'

Lechlade had pretensions of being a port. It took its role as the end of the recommended navigation seriously and modelled itself on a place of embarkation and arrival, rather like Zanzibar did. I imagined Lechlade would be a place where boats were bought and sold, where you could have a tattoo done if you felt like it, where watermen sitting in the corners of bars would tell stories of the river that would make you go out and check your knots. I imagined I'd meet the sort of people who'd give me first-hand advice on the stream ahead – on the perils of Hannington Bridge and the Sargasso Sea of Water Eaton, not the mention the route to the true source of the river.

But Lechlade isn't like that. It's a neat, well-swept, well-weeded, well-behaved town with a Lloyds Bank, a Barclays Bank, a Shell garage and a BP garage, and a Londis supermarket.

But the church in Lechlade is beautiful. It's weathered and worn and one's eyes climb slowly to its clock. Shelley, who rowed up to Lechlade from London in 1815, was inspired to pen 'Summer Evening in a Churchyard' here. The line 'Here could I hope, like some inquiring child sporting on graves, that death did hide from human sight sweet secrets' was printed on a plaque in the churchyard. Jennifer and I stood gazing at it. There was a chill in the air again. Jennifer said: ' "Or beside its breathless sleep that loveliest dreams perpetual watch did keep." '

'What's that?' I asked.

'The next line of the poem.'

'It's lovely.'

Old leaves were crackling in the wind, caught amongst the tombstones. The new graves had flowers, the old ones had stagnant water in their vases with insects floating on top. But there was a sense of celebration in the churchyard as well as one of peace. I put my arm through Jennifer's and we walked between the graves. Jennifer suddenly stopped and said: 'Quick, give me a pen and paper, I've had an idea.'

I tore a page off my notebook. She scribbled for a moment, crossed out a bit and then scribbled some more. She paused for a moment then looked to the church spire and with a flourish finished the poem. She said: 'I'm thinking of putting together a volume of poetry inspired by this trip. *Poems on a Journey up the Thames*, I think I'll call it. Listen to this: "Last night I slept neath a willow tree while the mist crept into my head, this river is sucking us into its mouth, it's a beast that must be fed." What do you reckon?'

'It's good, it's good.'

'I like the metaphor of the river being an animal and we're being drawn towards its mouth, helplessly, as if we were addicted.'

'That's what I said to you the other night.'

'When?'

'When you first arrived. I said the river is like a drug.'

'No you didn't.'

'I did.'

'Are you saying this is your idea as well?'

'I'm not exactly saying that, I'm saying that I've had that idea.'

'But I've just written it.'

'Yes, I know. I'm not disputing that, I'm just saying I had that idea as well. It was the first thing that occurred to me on the river – the river is like opium, I put.'

'Listen, from now on, don't tell me your ideas and I won't tell you mine.'

We went into the supermarket. We bought pork chops, onions and garlic. We bought celery, parsley and fennel seeds. We bought oil, cider and cream. There were six people in the queue at the checkout. Jennifer said to them: 'Could I possibly go in front of you? I wouldn't ask but

I've only got six months to live and I want to make best use of my time.'

Back in the boat Jennifer got out Delia Smith and said: 'We're going to have stuffed pork chop with fennel; a birthday treat,' and she set about softening the onion and garlic and mixing them with the celery, parsley, fennel seeds and bread crumbs. As she worked Boogie came and sat next to her and gave her a wink.

Next she cut out a hole in the pork chop and packed the stuffing in, then dusted it with flour and placed it into the hot oil. Boogie licked his lips.

Then she poured the cider over the chop and let it simmer for thirty minutes. Boogie grinned as the smells filled the boat.

Jennifer was just about to pour on the cream topping when the telephone rang. She breathed in deeply, picked up the receiver and said: 'Eeurgh . . . That's disgusting!'

'What is?'

'Look what the little bastard has done all over my Vodaphone.'

I looked at it. It certainly was disgusting. 'Yes,' I said. 'He does have bouts of being vile. It's amazing how quickly you get used to it though.'

She threw the Vodaphone to the floor and screamed: 'That's put me right off my food, that has,' and quick as a flash Boogie grabbed one of the pork chops and leapt out of the boat.

Jennifer screamed. Some coots paddling nearby ran for cover. She screamed again and the curtains were pulled back in *Maid Mind your own Business* across the water. She cried: 'I hate dogs. I really hate dogs. In fact . . .' and here she hesitated, 'I'm a cat person! I've never told you this but I'm a cat person! I like cats! I hate dogs! Understand. I hate dogs!'

There was a silence. The water slapped on the mahogany. An owl made a noise like a duck. I backed away from Jennifer. Boogie stuck his head back inside the canvas and looked at me with his 'did I just hear her right?' expression. There was an embarrassing silence, the first time I've ever had an embarrassing silence with Jennifer in the room.

Then she sniffed and said: 'Let's go and have lots to drink.'

We left Boogie behind and went to the Crown, then to the Red Lion, then to the New Inn and then to the Swan. In the Swan we had a meal: cheese and herb crusted cottage pie. It was delicious. I said to the barman: 'This is delicious.'

'One of Delia Smith's,' he said. 'Comes from that *One is Fun!* book. I just multiply the ingredients by sixty-five.'

We went back to the Crown, then back to the New Inn, then back to the Red Lion, then back to the Swan. By the end of the evening Jennifer had had two arguments and swopped addresses with three people. We called in at the Red Lion for a last one before closing time.

The bar was packed. A party of bright young things wearing clothing from Next surrounded the bar. One of them called out: 'Jennifer! Jennifer Conway?'

'Ray!' shrieked Jennifer and threw her arms around a man with a square head and a shirt with a green banana pattern. Then she pulled me over and said: 'Come and meet Ray.'

Ray was horrible, so were Fliss, Michele, Clive and Dominic. They were down for a wedding. 'There was a marquee and we all got blotto,' said Clive, who had a video camera.

Jennifer told them I'd rowed from London and Michele said: 'We rode from London too, we rode in Dominic's Cabriolet.' I suddenly wanted to be back on the river, moored to a meadow miles from anywhere. I started to miss the anonymity of the electricity pylons. Then Jennifer said: 'Let's all go back to the boat and have a party. It's Mark's birthday!'

They all insisted on singing happy birthday to me as we walked through the town. Clive filmed the occasion. I felt a real prat, Jennifer put her arm around me and I said: 'Who are these people?'

'They're a laugh, aren't they? I can't stand them. But I like lots of people I can't stand. They are a laugh though.' As she spoke I noticed Ray was walking down the street and changing round the notes in the milk bottles on the doorsteps.

When we reached *Maegan* they all said what a beautiful boat she was. Clive filmed her from three sides. Jennifer proudly swept back the canvas flap and said: 'C'mon in, folks; make yourself at home.'

We piled in and I lit the lamp and there at the back of the boat was Boogie with his legs wrapped round the hind quarters of one of Lechlade's least virtuous bitches. Michele screamed. Ray said: 'That's disgusting.' Clive said: 'What's he doing?' but didn't stop filming. And Dominic said: 'Whatever he's doing, he's doing it all over your sleeping bag.' Jennifer clambered up the boat, picked up her wok and belted Boogie over the head with it. It made a noise like a bell. Boogie and his girlfriend leapt out and brought down the tent. Jennifer stood alone in the stern covered in green canvas. She began to cry. 'He's spoiled my birthday party!' she sobbed.

'It was my birthday party!' I said.

'I don't care whose birthday party it is; he's spoiled it, like he spoils everything else. I've had enough. That's it! Either he goes or I go!' And she appeared from under the canvas in a rage. I wasn't so sure her short hair suited her now. She said: 'I'm going to make some telephone calls.

When I come back I expect you to have had him put down,' and she grapped her Vodaphone and strode off.

There was a silence amongst the rest of us. Clive, who didn't like silences, said they ought to go home but that he had the whole episode on film and we should all go round to his house one day and watch it. They left. I was suddenly on my own. Then from the back yard of the nearby tea room Boogie appeared. We went for a long walk along the towpath.

'The country is the place, you know, Boogie. The country is the place folks like you and I should live.'

Boogie licked something off a No Mooring sign.

'The trouble is I work in the city. But you? You could live anywhere. I mean, wouldn't you like to move out to a nice home in the country?' Boogie sat down and scratched his ear even more violently than before.

'Maybe it would be better if you were to stay in the country.' He stopped and gave me his 'typical! Well, just give me my can opener, mate. No need to worry about me' expression.

'Now c'mon. Be fair,' I said. 'What can I do? I know she appears unreasonable but I've got myself to think of. It's either you or her. It's an impossible situation. You'll be all right. You make friends easy.'

We walked a long way that night. When we got back to the boat Jennifer was in bed. I got in quietly beside her and touched her arm. She didn't turn to me; she just said: 'I feel desperate sometimes.'

I said: 'I know what you mean. I used to feel like that sometimes too. But since I've been on the river I've felt different. I feel the river flowing through me now like blood. All things change but the river keeps on rolling. Things are a lot clearer now. I can look at my life from a distance. I can feel the force of a natural flow in all that

I do. And there's an inevitability about everything. I see now that birth and death are irrevocably linked.'

She turned over and said: 'Why have you been talking such inane rubbish the last few days?'

'I don't know,' I said.

I had a vivid dream that night. I dreamt Delia Smith was in the back of the boat. She was wearing a black velvet evening dress and a sparkling tiara and she was cooking the most glorious meals for one then eating them all herself. She was angry with me. She offered me a glass of wine but it had a dead beetle floating upside down in it.

I woke with a start. In the moonlight I could see Boogie crawling out of *Maegan* and up on to the bank. A lump came to my throat. What a noble dog this was, and I was witnessing his finest hour. Like Captain Oates he was sacrificing himself so that the expedition to the source could continue. He could sense this was not a happy party. To end the conflict he knew there was only one course of action to take.

He walked off into the meadow. I called softly: 'Goodbye, Boogie. And thank you.' He stopped and turned. A car's headlights flashed in his eye, and in his mouth I saw a white object. At first I thought it was a bone but then I realized it was a Vodaphone.

He buried it, then trotted back to the boat, stuffed his nose under his tail and went back to sleep.

10. Meet Me at the Source if You Like

In the history of exploration there is one man who towers above all others in the department of portage. He is Charles Sturt, an explorer with conviction if ever there was one, a man so sure that a country as vast as Australia could not possibly have such a poor water supply, that when he set out from Adelaide in 1844 in search of an inland sea, he took a boat with him.

I thought of Charles Sturt a lot over the next two days as I made my quest for Cricklade. He was an inspiration. He even managed to inspire me to take a jog the morning I left Lechlade, although after I'd run a hundred yards or so I felt silly and walked back to the boat. I felt drained from the previous forty-eight hours. But I also felt nervous and wanted to get moving. I knew from here on I would need to have my wits about me, from here on I would need to try to put aside all that had happened and concentrate my mind, from here on I was on my own again.

I doused my head with river water, and looked at my reflection. I had bags under my eyes. So did Boogie. He sat expressionless on the back seat. 'I understand,' I said and patted him. Presently the sun blasted through the mist and glinted off an ice-cream sign across the river. Lechlade tremored with church bells and I stripped down to my shorts and hat, and set off. Boogie, as if sensing the gravity of the moment, positioned himself on the stern, casting a cold, discerning eye upstream, seemingly alert to all the dangers ahead, actually alert to not a single one of them.

Our last contact with the civilized river was at the Inglesham Roundhouse where the abandoned Thames Severn Canal met the Thames. This link between London and Bristol was the first canal project to excite investors when news of Leonardo da Vinci's lock reached these shores at the beginning of the seventeenth century. So excited were they that a hundred and fifty years later they actually got round to building the thing. But it was beset with problems from the start, and as canals nationwide became more efficient, traders realized the Thames was a slow waterway and were reluctant to use it. The owners worked hard at bringing the navigation up to standard, finally turning it into an efficient route around about the same time that railways were invented. The rest is a predictable story of decline, and in 1933 all was abandoned.

The Inglesham Roundhouse – one of a series of buildings along the canal built as watch-houses for the lock-keeper – stood at the junction of the canal with the Thames and the river Coln. I'd seen many fine and beautiful houses on the river over the previous hundred miles, but this Roundhouse with its cottage hiding amongst a veil of willows was the most appealing of them all. It was all chimneys and vines and seemed a wonderful place to be born, grow up in and then come back to. It was more like a nest than a house. I looked hard but couldn't see a burglar alarm.

The house and the hamlet of Inglesham disappeared behind a bend and ahead of me was nothing but sky and field. Immediately the river narrowed and shallowed. For the first time I could see the bottom. No dredger had ever come up here, and without traffic the weeds and reeds flourished and soon grew out of control. It would have been possible just to force a passage, but I hated doing this, the coots built their nests on precarious platforms amongst the reeds and more than once when I pushed my way through I had ended up staring into the forlorn faces of five chicks whose home I had just bulldozed.

By now though I was useful with my sculls. I could turn *Maegan* on a lilypad and twist her through the narrowest inlet. The struggles I'd had coming under Maidenhead Bridge and through Hennerton Backwater now proved their worth as I picked and paddled a course through the obstacles.

I saw only a lone canoeist all day. He looked at me strangely and wouldn't have stopped had I not called out to him. I wanted encouragement more than anything, but he said: 'Cricklade? You'll be lucky, you're too heavy. You'll never make Castle Eaton Bridge,' and he wriggled his hips and swerved through the reeds like a water snake and was gone.

I kept going while the sun reached for the top of the sky. There was no shade here; this was wild country and for the first time on this trip I felt completely committed. At Hannington Bridge were the first shallows. I leapt out and felt the water fill my wellingtons, and I cringed as I dragged the boat over the river bed and the gravel scored *Maegan*'s belly.

But I had a different kind of energy that day. At one point when the sun was high, I remember I came to a mound of gravel that seemed like an unbreachable barrier, and the effort to haul *Maegan* over too much. But I closed my eyes and thought back over the previous three days, and I saw Jennifer standing there with her fists clenched, shrieking. I grunted and tugged and the boat rode over. Afterwards, I leant over the gunwales panting, and Boogie eyed me approvingly. He hadn't moved from the back

seat since Lechlade. He'd won his battle and he wasn't
going to give his position up for anyone.

I slipped past the mysterious village of Kempsford
where the banks were high and vegetation thick and I
could only see the church tower and some rooftops. I was
beginning to feel what life on the river was like without
other boats. I felt an isolation that was unnerving because
it had a urgency to it, and the urgency mounted each
bend I took – around the next corner there might be an
obstruction that would end the journey there and then.

Now the river was only fifteen feet wide in places and
the banks grew high and claustrophobic. I could no longer
find the depth or width to use the sculls so I stood on the
bow and paddled as the reeds grew more and more dense.

Then as the day cooled the water became clearer. Whenever I jumped in to haul *Maegan* I could see minnows
gathered round my knees. And the shallows were so fre-
quent now I was hauling more then paddling. It was as I
was bent forward, heaving, with the rope over my
shoulder, that I turned a corner and saw before me Castle
Eaton Bridge.

It was an ugly metal structure, green, although the
setting sun gave it a rusted effect. I paused and pulled my
hat down. The river widened here and there was depth
and room to manoeuvre, so I decided to take a run at the
bridge. I climbed back in the boat, steadied myself and
pulled away. Castle Eaton church flashed past. A very
pleasant riverside pub called the Red Lion with a number
of people in its garden flashed past. They called out to me
but I kept going, I think I might even have given them a
look of grim determination. I navigated the arch success-
fully but so fine had I cut it I had to pull my sculls in and
I found myself leaning on my boat hook desperately trying
to push my way past the rapids and into the safety of the
pool I could see beyond. I pushed with mighty effort,

lunged for another rock to support myself, missed, slipped and tumbled out of the boat, and I was under the water with an iciness in my ears.

I was only submerged for a second but it was long enough to savour the experience; it was like a baptism. I surfaced, clutching my binoculars, to find myself in three foot of fast-moving water and I remember standing there and thinking how, despite the effort, there had been a strange peace over the river all day.

A cygnet came paddling towards me, screaming pathetically, presumably searching for its mother. But no adult was anywhere to be found. I smiled at the helpless-ness of the thing, and couldn't believe how such a graceless chick could ever turn into a swan. I looked at it through my binoculars and it dived into some reeds, in tears. That was when I noticed *Maegan* had vanished. I scratched my hat.

'Hello,' said a voice from the bridge. I looked up to see a woman with a napkin tucked into her front. She said: 'Is that your boat?'

'What boat?'

'That boat that just came under the bridge. It's yours, isn't it?'

'Umm. Might be mine, did it have a dog onboard?'

'We were watching you from the pub garden. We were having supper. Then your dog came running into the pub. It was as if he was trying to tell us something. He probably thought you were in mortal danger and he was trying to save your life. We've given him something to eat, is that all right?'

I waded out of the river and she offered me her hand and helped me up the bank.

'You're wet,' she said.

'You've got pickle on your lip,' I replied.

'Did you fall in?'

'No, no. There's a cygnet down there I was studying. It's lost, I think. Did you know that swans keep the same mate for the whole of their lives?'

She led me to the other side of the bridge. 'There's your boat,' she said. *Maegan* was wedged in some willow stumps downstream.

'And there's your dog,' she added. Boogie was in the pub garden, not a drop of water on him. He was sat in front of the woman's husband being fed mouthfuls of quiche.

I joined them. Her husband said: 'Did you fall in?'

'He was looking at the baby swan,' said his wife.

'Wildlife expert are you?' said the husband.

'Well . . .'

'I knew someone like you, into animals. He wanted to study elks. He wanted to live with them. He wasn't odd or anything, he just liked elks. He tried everything to convince them he was one of them. He strapped antlers to his head. He ran around the forest on all fours. He moaned like an elk. No good at all. Then one day he got up really close to a grazing herd, and he started to eat leaves. And you know what?'

'What?'

'They all pissed off, ran a mile. He packed up after that. It wasn't worth the effort, he said. "I don't like elks that much," were his words. That's a nice boat. Travelling on your own?'

'No, well, my girlfriend had to go home. She had an accident.'

'Nothing serious I hope?'

'It's a long story.'

Actually it was a short story. I was woken that morning as the tent was ripped off and there stood Jennifer looking very worried. I'd never seen her so distraught. She was rummaging round the bowels of the boat, throwing lug-

gage on to the bank, scrambling about in the bilges. I
said: 'What is it?' And she looked up at me with mud on
her face and a breathlessness: 'I can't find my Vodaphone.
It's just disappeared. I always have it next to me where I
sleep but it's gone.'

I lay there. 'Well don't help me find it, will you?' she
said. She was losing her cool. I'd seen her angry before
but her anger, though venomous, was always controlled.
I looked round for Boogie. He was sniffing about on the
quay, licking the petrol pump by the marina. For a moment I thought what I'd seen during the night had been
a dream but now I remembered. Boogie had at last found
Jennifer's soft underbelly and had gone right for it. I
wanted to tell her but I couldn't. I just couldn't.

She cleared the boat in exasperation. Her eyes were
wild, and she said: 'Right! There's nothing else for it.'
And she composed herself and from her bag pulled out a
black suit, a pair of black stockings and a pair of black
patent leather shoes. She dressed there on the lawn in front
of the tea shop, then she grabbed her handbag, took out
her credit cards and threw the rest on the ground: 'I've
got to go,' she said.

'Go where?'

'Back.'

'Back where?'

'To work!'

I said: 'Jennifer. Before you go, just tell me one thing.
What exactly is it that you do?'

She shook her head, and strode off. I called out: 'Maybe
I'll see you at the source.' But she didn't respond. She
passed the petrol pump without looking at Boogie and
that was the last I saw of her.

That evening I sat in the boat under the lamp glow as
military aircraft hummed overhead. I prepared sautéed
fennel with Parmesan followed by egg and anchovy salad

with herbs. Now Jennifer was gone it was just Delia and me again.

There was no towpath to the river now so later I took Boogie for a walk in the Castle Eaton churchyard. Confetti lay on the ground. An owl squeaked and Boogie licked something off a gravestone. 'I feel the trip is reaching a climax,' I said. 'I feel as though something is about to happen. You know you've ruined my chances with Jennifer for good now, don't you?'

We reached the river at the bottom of the churchyard. It was hurrying, like a child learning to run, having to keep going to stay upright. But it learned fast. You could throw a rock in the water here and it would have an immediate effect – a rapid would form and the current would divert – but by the morning the river would have compensated somewhere further downstream.

Back in *Maegan* I lay awake in my sleeping bag. I felt as though I should have had a lot to think about but I only wanted to occupy myself with the source. Boogie lay in the back of the boat with his eyes on me. I briefly wondered if his look was one of an animal with an uneasy conscience. But I quickly dismissed that idea.

Outside the reeds rustled and inside I lay dreaming. Delia Smith was sat in the back of the boat, cooking, cooking, cooking, surrounding herself with stacks of pancakes, and growing fatter and fatter. She was adding everything she could find to a stir-fry. All of Jennifer's luggage: her shoes, her books, her plants. They all went into the wok. Then she leaned over and tried to grab my wellingtons. I woke panting and sweating. A Nimrod enemy surveillance aircraft droned overhead.

The following day was just as hot. The heat shimmered above the dry ploughed earth, and there was a taste of dust in the air. The level of the river fluctuated from

six foot to six inches without warning. At one point I
remembered what Mark Edwards had said, and built a
flash-lock out of rocks. And once, where it was possible
to excavate the gravel, I dug a channel with Jennifer's
wok. But these were mere interruptions. As I came to the
area known as Water Eaton I met a far more serious
obstacle, and found myself faced with something I'd
always steered clear of on this trip – a showdown with
the local swans.

I'd seen a number the previous day. But they'd retreated
whenever I grew close. On this occasion there were only
half a dozen birds to start with, but then from the reeds
and the bushes and the air a whole squadron formed,
about twenty-five birds. They blocked the passage, and
this time it was clear they were going to stand their
ground.

On the main river the swans were used to the boats and
I could negotiate with them and slowly manoeuvre round
them. But in these parts they were unused to interference
and to being frightened. They were masters of the river
and instinctively unafraid of all around them. So I stopped
and squinted at them, waiting for a sign. But none came.
They seemed nervous, paddling in between each other in
a confused manner. I edged forward. They waited until I
was within thirty feet of them, then suddenly took action.
In pairs they rose up and came running along the water
straight at me, wings drawn and thrashing, mouths open
and hissing. Boogie dived under the seat. I picked up the
wok ready to defend myself. But, just before they reached
me, one by one with the greatest effort, they somehow
managed to haul themselves into the air and clear the
boat. I ducked as their shadows covered me and their
undercarriages just cleared my head. They took off in
waves like bomber aircraft. The sound was one of stretching muscle and physical stress. It was painful to watch.

For five minutes they kept coming, each following the example of the other, their wing tips touching, their necks straining forward. And then as soon as they were airborne they were caught on the stiff breeze and had no option but to bank and be blown downwind over the treetops.

Only one bird remained. It trod the water with one foot, the other lay embedded in its down. I waited for it to follow the others but it made no effort. To begin with I wondered if it was injured, but it was simply more inquisitive than the rest. I remember looking at it and thinking how it reminded me of Jennifer, elegant, aloof, assertive and with a long neck. For the first time I noticed a vulnerability in swans, and I realized I was coming to change my opinion of them. Having spent so long on the river I didn't find them as arrogant as before. It was dawning on me that all they'd ever done was treat me as an equal. I pulled a piece of bread from my loaf, broke it in pieces and proffered them on my hand. The swan lifted its head and turned a circle. I was drifting away from it but it followed me, and came closer until it could reach my palm. *Maegan* hit the bank and stopped and the swan leant forward and took the bread and I felt a thrill as its beak brushed my wrist. It swallowed the gift then leant forward for more, I reached for the packet and that's when Boogie stuck his head through my legs and the swan rose like a cobra. I shouted at Boogie who barked at the swan and the bird spat and hissed and tore off downstream. Boogie looked at me with his 'I've just saved your life; what have you got to say about that?' expression.

I pressed on. There was no channel now and *Maegan* had to carve a passage through the weed like an icebreaker; I pushed and pulled her for most of the day. At one point I decided progress was impossible and that I would have to stop where I was. It was unbearable to think that I should fail at this last hurdle; I'd already gone under Crick-

lade bypass and could see a housing estate. But I couldn't
haul the boat over rocks. I needed a boost, and fittingly,
it was Boogie who provided one. On this stretch he had
spent most of the time in the river, partly because he'd
taken to water now, but largely because I'd decided at the
first shallows that I was damned if I was going to haul
Maegan with him lying on the back seat, and so I'd thrown
him out.

He was a little ahead of the boat knee-deep in water,
when, suddenly, he disappeared under the surface. He
came up coughing and covered in slime and I pulled him
in to the bank and hugged him. He'd found a deep-water
passage just when we needed it.

We continued as insects swarmed around the boat and
creepers hung from the willows and coiled themselves
around me. Then, from round a bend I heard voices,
young voices with a heavy Wiltshire accent. I looked
on in disbelief as two young boys appeared in a plastic
dinghy.

'Hello,' they said.

'What are you doing here? You shouldn't be here!' I
sounded incredulous.

'Why not?'

'Because this is an impossible stretch of river that most
men fear.'

'We're paddling down to Lechlade.'

'From where?'

'Cricklade. We live on the estate. We're going to see
our uncle. We often do it.'

And they were gone, gliding smoothly over the gravel
with the current. They were about nine years old.

So! I thought. The local natives use this as a route to
Lechlade. They've had to devise a special craft and they
only send the young among them, but it is a viable
passage.

Further encouragement came that afternoon when I saw a couple sitting in a field. I waved and shouted: 'How far to Cricklade?'

'A mile,' he said.

'More like three,' she said.

'It's a dump, anyway,' he said.

But I wasn't really bothered. I'd just seen the incentive I needed: the spire of Cricklade parish church poking up through the hedgerows like a finishing post, a mile away, no more.

I hauled the boat on past the back gardens and garages of Cricklade and into the town. In the distance I could see High Bridge with some kids sitting on top. I shouted to them and they were in the river with me helping me haul *Maegan* over the last fifty yards, singing and screaming as they pulled and pushed. Some members of the local cricket team took off their shoes, rolled up their whites and joined in. We manoeuvred *Maegan* to the bridge and I slumped over her exhausted. 'I've sculled this boat 130 miles uphill,' I said to one of the cricketers, and he replied: 'That's nothing, we lost by eight wickets this afternoon. Are you coming to the pub?'

'Yes,' I said. And when I got there I bought myself a Babycham.

It was an evening to remember. I told them of the trials I'd had coming under Hannington Bridge and of the wild swans of Water Eaton, and they told me of their slip fielder who had had twenty-four chances so far this season and dropped the lot. I told them of my ducking at Castle Eaton and how if it hadn't been for the wok I might not have made it, and they told me how their number eight batsman had once played for England, although not at cricket. Then I popped the all-important question: I told them of my quest for the source of the river and asked if anyone of them had any idea where it was? And they thought about this for a moment and then told me about their second change seamer who was the spitting image of the pope.

Later on though, I was sitting at a table with the wicket keeper when he said: 'I heard you talking about the source of the Thames earlier.'

'That's right.'

'Well, I know where it is.'

'Where?'

He looked at his empty glass, and grinned. I bought him another pint and he leant over the table and said quietly: 'It's near Kemble village at Trewsbury Mead, ten miles from here.'

I'd heard so many conflicting stories since London that it was tempting to treat him as just one more man in a corner of a pub, but he had a gleam of truth in his eye. I said: 'What evidence do you base this theory on?'

'I've seen it with my own eyes. I farm round there. I'd lost a calf one day. I was walking through the fields looking for it and suddenly I stumbles across a ring of stones. There was no water or nothing, just an ash tree inscribed with two initials, almost swallowed by the bark – the initials TH.'

'What does TH mean?'

'Thames Head.'

I gasped. It all slotted into place now.

'There was another clue there as well,' said the wicket keeper.

'What?'

'Right next to the tree there was a bloody great plaque that said: "This is the source of the Thames." '

After the pub shut I took Boogie a walk through the town. I felt satisfied. We stood on High Bridge and I looked downstream at the thin leg of water, and I smiled

when I thought of the great expanse of river on which I'd
started the journey.

The street light danced on the stream, and there in the
trees I noticed a supermarket trolley. No one was looking
so I clambered down on to the bank and pushed it in the
water. The sensation was minimal. So I pulled it out and
tried again – still nothing. I tried once more and derived
no thrill or pleasurable feeling of any description. Despite
all the talk, pushing supermarket trolleys into rivers is a
pointless exercise.

Cricklade was unlike any other town I'd passed through.
One reason was because it hadn't one familiar shop-front
on the whole street, but it was also different because it
was untouched by the river. I heard talk of a scheme to
make the Thames navigable up from Lechlade, to install
three more locks, and dredge it and so attract the pleasure
craft, but talk was all it was, and the stream that was
the Thames passed without interest through Cricklade. It
wanted nothing to do with the town, and no one in the
town had any use for it. If anything the river was a
nuisance. The farmers laid gravel over it to create a cattle
crossing.

This gave the town a different appeal because, unlike
Marlow, Henley and Wallingford, it didn't need to flaunt
its riparian status. It had wide streets and a wealthy past
as a wool merchants' town and it could depend on its
parochial qualities. If anything it reminded me more of a
seaside town. The High Street climbed a hill at such an
angle it looked as though you would find a cliff at the
top.

I was up early the following morning and found a cafe.
My plan for the day was simple enough but conditions
would be different from here on. Now I was on foot
rather than in the boat, and the river wouldn't dominate

the countryside the way it had. Now it would sneak
through fields; it could disappear into a patch of brambles
and not come out again. The wicket keeper had told me
that to get to the ash tree I must keep to the main channel
no matter how small it became and no matter how many
other streams tried to lead me away. There'd be times
when the river was almost dry, he warned me, but I
mustn't be deceived.

I had a fried breakfast and read a paper whilst all around
me were conversations about the scout club and the rent
rebates, the kind of conversations I'd not heard since
London; conversations that didn't once mention the local
regatta or the cost of overnight mooring or the journey
time from Paddington. I was out of the commuter belt
for the first time and it was like falling asleep on a train
and waking up in a different country.

'Eggs, bacon and beans!'

'Thank you.'

I ate my plateful and wiped it up with some bread. It
was time to get moving. Outside, Boogie was having his
name taken by a local policeman.

I followed the river bank out of town. Fences had been
put across the water by farmers to act as stock barriers,
but there were fishermen's paths to follow.

I quickly came to the confluence with the River Churn,
a sizeable piece of water but, like the Evenlode, the Coln
and the Windrush before it, the Thames spat it out and
continued.

Far more impressive was the stream I found just before
Ashton Keynes. By this time the Thames was just a trickle
and so I followed the larger body of water until I came
to a bridge. A man with a shotgun leant over it.

'What sort of dog is that?' he said.

'Russian dalmatian.'

'Thought so.' He tried to change the subject, but he was having problems so I helped him. I said: 'Is that your car?' indicating the beautifully restored 1958 Morris Cowley by the roadside. It had been resprayed in its original light grey. The chrome had been dipped, the leather re-upholstered, the tyres painted. It was pristine.

'No,' he said.

There was another silence which we both felt comfortable with. This trip had taught me how to meet all sorts of interesting people and then not say anything to them. I felt a drop of rain. An aircraft flew low overhead. I trained my binoculars on it and spotted a pilot with black hair, a blue pullover and glasses.

Presently my friend said: 'You walking?'

'Yes. I'm following the river Thames.'

'No, you're not.'

'Yes, I am.'

'No, you're not. You're following the Swill Brook. That's the Thames back there.'

'But it's nothing but a ditch.'

'May look like a ditch but that's because the gravel pits drain it. You go into the village and you'll find ducks and everything swimming about. You can trust me, I'm a local character.'

So I retraced my steps and followed the ditch into Ashton Keynes and sure enough by the time the stream had passed the churchyard it had swelled to a size where I could have sculled on it again had I been with *Maegan*. I sent a postcard to my grandmother and continued through a blue haze of dragonflies.

By early afternoon the skies grew full of cold black cloud and my pace was quickening. Boogie seemed uneasy. In Somerford Keynes he had a fight with a rockery and the rockery came off better. He drank frequently from the river; it was as if he knew it was going to run dry soon.

It was crystal clear and sprinkled with white crowfoot, but it had degenerated to a dribble.

Another railway bridge and another main road and then the water was motionless, barely deep enough for a resident family of moorhens to splash about in. A hundred yards further and it disappeared into the ground. If I squeezed the earth water rose to the surface, but the river was gone and for the first time in almost three weeks there were no reflections around me, just a bright green dampness.

I followed a dry groove in the earth which was presumably flooded under wetter conditions. It led me past the distant spire of Kemble church, then under the Fosse Way and through a long meadow until ahead I could see a tree. I peered through my binoculars – a crow standing quite happily on a fence took off and vanished. I focused and recognized the distinctive leaves of an ash. And there beneath it was a ring of white stones. I strode on and reached the source of the River Thames at 3.30 in the afternoon of 28 May 1988.

It was an unimpressive setting really, just nettles, some dung and the dry cracked earth. There was supposed to be a spring beneath the stones, but they didn't look as though they'd seen water for years. I'd love to have found a coot's nest or a willow stump there, instead there was the plaque, proclaiming this spring in Trewsbury Mead as the true source of the great river. Boogie cocked his leg on it.

I stood there in reverence for a minute or two until I was disturbed by voices coming through the woods. A party of people climbed over a stile and walked through the field. As they came closer I could hear they were speaking German. They marched up to me and their spokesman said: 'We are looking for the source of the Thames.'

It started to rain. We were all standing in the middle of a field in Gloucestershire with our anoraks over our heads.

'Look no further,' I said.

'This is it?'

'Yep. And I was here first.'

They looked around. One voice said: 'Aber wo ist die Wasser?' And the spokesman said: 'But where is the water? We have come all the way from London and there is no water. I thought there would be a Little Chef or a Pay and Display at least but there is nothing. Are you sure this is the source?'

'Sure.'

'How did you get here?'

'I sculled.'

'You what?'

'I rowed.'

'Oh! You are *Three Men in a Boat* to say nothing of the dog. But where are the other two? My favourite bit is when Harris sings the song and can't remember the words. Why are you looking strangely? We have been travelling from London with nothing but Radio One for amusement. It took us two hours in a Toyota minibus. What a waste of time. My name is Felix.'

From somewhere Boogie appeared with a steak sandwich in his mouth.

'It is all right for the dog, isn't it?' said Felix.

11. I'll See You Sometime

I sculled back to Oxford in the rain. With the aid of the current it only took a few days. I just pulled my hat down and went as fast as I could.

One day the mist didn't lift at all. The river was cocooned in a cloud. Military aircraft on their low-level flying manoeuvres blasted overhead but I was blind to them. There were no other boats on the water, no people on the towpath. I travelled with my head down. *Maegan* knew the channel. All I remember noticing during those few days was that the dandelions were over, their white seeds scattered on the water. On this journey I'd seen them flourish, flower and die and now their ashes were strewn.

I got going each morning at first light when the river mist crept into the tent and dampened my covers. And I kept going until the daylight died and the crusts on my hands had dried on the sculls. I felt sedated. I stopped noticing the country I was passing through. But this had never been a scenically startling journey. The Thames was a steady river that dripped and flowed, hardly tripping up once on its way to the sea. Its influence was a subliminal one. I remember stopping one night in a pub called the Rose Revived. I sat at the bar and heard the barmaid talking to a customer about holidays, and how the destinations never lived up to expectations. She said: 'I went

up the Nile the year before last. I didn't enjoy it. The
pyramids just aren't worth the bother. The pictures on
the postcards were wonderful but the real things are a
disappointment.'

And the customer nodded and said: 'I know what you
mean. The same thing happened to me with those foun-
tains in Rome.'

The Thames conjures up castles and palaces and royal
barges and regattas and a voyage through the history of
England. And it is all of these things somewhere along
the route, there's even a gorge or two, but it's essentially
coots and willows and the plop of the chub and the knowledge that you're never far from a branch of Boots. On
discovering the source to be a dry patch of ground in a
field I wasn't surprised or disappointed. The idea of it
spouting out of a lake over falls just wasn't suitable. The
Thames is a civilized river and above such sensationalism.
It inspires tranquillity and self-reflection rather than
derring-do and getting up before eight for a swim.

Back in London I lay low for a while. I wanted to call Jennifer and tell her the task had been completed, but I felt
uncomfortable about the whole thing. Not long after I'd
been back my friend Sarah called round. She wanted me to
look after her goldfish while she went away. I said to
her: 'I thought you'd just been away, to South America?'

'I'm moving out there for a while. I've been offered the
managership of the new branch of Sketchley's in Montevi-
deo. It's promotion. So how was your trip?'

'It was good . . . It was good.'

'Did you find the source of the Thames?'

'Yes, indeed. I solved the mystery surrounding the
source of that great river.'

'Well . . . ?'

'Well what?'

'Well where is it?'

'You'll laugh when I tell you.'

'Yes?'

'Well . . . the source of the Thames is in Trewsbury Mead, a field just over the A433 south of Cirencester.'

'Isn't that where most people thought it was?'

'Er . . . yes.'

'. . .'

'And . . . so . . . so the trip has been a resounding success, insomuch as I have proved most people are correct in their opinion as to where the Thames rises.'

'I see,' said Sarah. 'Listen, feeding instructions are on the packet,' and she handed me the fish bowl.

Most people were similarly impressed, and yet I couldn't help but feel it was a hollow success. The problem was I could see little of worth had come out of the journey. At one point I hoped it might have been of scientific value as research into the use of dogs on long river expeditions, but reading through my notes the only conclusion they reach is that dogs are of no use at all – they inspire people to say boring things to you from the bank.

But the rewards of a journey aren't always immediate and aren't always manifest. The point is should we count milestones or miles? And the truth is I learned a lot from my time on the river – learned a lot, that is, about myself.

This may not sound so special. After all, most journeys offer travellers an insight into their own personality. But the difference between this trip and any other I've been on is that although I know I did learn a lot about myself, now I'm back I can't for the life of me remember what it was. As soon as I left the river its spirit drained away from me. The morning I woke up in bed again I no longer felt that insouciance the river inspired. I suddenly felt responsible again. It was as if I'd been addicted to something then suddenly forgot what the addiction was.

And that's rather how I feel about Jennifer now. I think her problem was she was fighting the river all the time rather than trying to harness its energy. Even Boogie could sense this, and he knew it was a weakness. She was rigid. I remember when she said: 'Coots are fun to watch but they aren't very efficient animals. They could be far more productive. Ergonomically, they're a disaster. I'd never employ one,' it was clear she wasn't ever going to be a waterwoman.

But I should have realized this beforehand. And while I can blame all sorts of people and animals for what happened, I know I'm liable as well. It didn't dawn on me in time that Jennifer isn't impressed by men who try to impress her. I imagined someone so inaccessible could be reached somehow. There had to be a key to her, a secret channel no one had ever taken before, a backwater through which her defences could be breached. But treating her like a river was my downfall, and I know now that even if we had reached the source together there would have been nowhere else for us to go but back downstream. Boogie may have realized this. His actions, though vulgar to an unacceptable degree, may have been with the best intentions. He may have seen the lack of communication between Jennifer and me. He may have noted the lack of negotiation, the lack of genuine affection, the lack of trust between us. He may have noticed my infatuation and decided he had to take the initiative. He may have decided Jennifer was coming between him and me. He may have seen the link between man and dog threatened and the expedition put in jeopardy as a consequence. In the end honour may have forced him to act. I'd like to think so. But he probably behaved the way he did because he can't stand pseuds.

I haven't seen or even spoken to Jennifer since. I called

her office and her PA answered and said: 'May I ask who's calling?'

'Mark Wallington.'

'What company?'

'Personal call.'

'I'm sorry, Ms Conway is on the other line at the moment, can I ask what it's about?'

'Yes. I'd like to know her opinion on where our relationship stands at the moment and what, if any, effect she feels the time we had together on the river had on our future. I feel that I spent too long competing for her rather than against her which was patronizing on my behalf I know, but I feel that if she analyses her own behaviour she will come to see that she was lacking in the essential skills needed to be a travelling companion. Before we went on this trip I would have travelled to the ends of the earth with her. I still would but now I think I'd be tempted to leave her there. Maybe she'd like to meet for a drink sometime and talk it over. I've got plans to climb a mountain. I've also got her handbag and her wok. Tell her to call me when she gets time.'

'I told you it would all end in . . .'

'Yes, yes, I know you told me.'

But she hasn't called yet. Not many people do call when you're writing a book. They think you don't want to be interrupted. And then whenever the phone does go and I say I'm writing about a rowing trip up the Thames, everyone says 'Oh, you mean *Three Men in a Boat*.' At first I gave my rehearsed response, about how my book and *Three Men in a Boat* have nothing in common, that the river has changed beyond recognition in a hundred years, and it's stupid to imagine I could re-create such a trip. But I don't bother now. I chuckle and say: 'Well, yes I suppose so.' I think people prefer it that way. I've even tried to convince myself. I say to myself: 'It doesn't matter about the motorboats and the housing estates and the branches of Waitrose and Pizzaland, these changes to the Thames are all peripheral. The river itself is as languid and as oblivious as it ever was, as timeless as Jerome's book.' I'm not sure about this though.

I have, however, discovered one similarity between Jerome's book and mine, and that is they were both written in the summer time, in a room at the top of the house, looking out over London. And I think I feel closer to him because of this than anything to do with the Thames. I imagine him sitting in a room above the rooftops with pigeons pattering over his tiles just as they do over mine. I look at them with my binoculars sometimes and they fly off and hide, so I turn my attention to the street. It's full of puddles, has been for most of the summer, and as the daylight fails the gas showroom is reflected in the pavement and I'm immediately taken back to the wonderful reflections of Cliveden Deep and of Pangbourne, of Mapledurham House and of Tadpole Bridge, and of the willows. It's at times like these that I know the only reason I can live in this city is that only occasionally does it remind me of the country.

This tenuous connection with Jerome was the excuse I sought and I no longer felt the need to distance myself from the man. In the autumn I even went back to the river to visit Ewelme in Oxfordshire where he's buried. I drove down there on a frosty Sunday morning. The village looked delightful and the church of St Mary's was frozen into place under the blue sky. A bonfire smoked over a wall, and the rooks' nests were clearly visible in the bare trees. I found Jerome's family plot not far away from the church door, his wife and daughter lying by his side. I'd read a biography of him during the summer and hadn't been surprised to find him hint at an ambivalence to his success. He wrote: 'I have written books that have

appeared to me more clever, books that have appeared to
me more humorous. But it is as the author of *Three Men
in a Boat (to say nothing of the Dog)* that the public persists
in remembering me.' I stood there for a couple of minutes
breathing a cloud. I just wanted to have a look.

After visiting the churchyard I walked Boogie down to
the river at Benson. Six months on and the ducklings
were having formation flying lessons. The immature coots
sat in the middle of the channel developing their bald
patches. The grebes were learning karate, and the cygnets
were no longer squat grey squirts. They'd lost their fluff
and grown their necks and turned into beautiful graceful
creatures with a natural vanity. Boogie looked confused
at first but then we walked along the towpath and slowly
he identified his surroundings. At one point a heron landed
near us and we stopped and watched it feed. And as the
bird's head dived into the water and emerged each time
with a fish in its beak, Boogie wagged his tail and grinned
and I was sure he was recalling our trip.

When we got home that night he stuck his face in the
fish bowl and ate Sarah's goldfish.

Bestselling Humour

☐ The Ascent of Rum Doodle	W E Bowman	£2.99
☐ Tim Brooke-Taylor's Golf Bag	Tim Brooke-Taylor	£3.99
☐ Shop! or A Store Is Born	Jasper Carrott	£2.99
☐ Cat Chat	Peter Fincham	£3.50
☐ Art of Coarse Drinking	Michael Green	£2.50
☐ Rambling On	Mike Harding	£2.50
☐ Sex Tips For Girls	Cynthia Heimel	£2.95
☐ Tales From Witney Scrotum	Peter Tinniswood	£2.50
☐ Tales From A Long Room	Peter Tinniswood	£2.75
☐ Uncle Mort's North Country	Peter Tinniswood	£2.50
☐ Five Hundred Mile Walkies	Mark Wallington	£2.50

Prices and other details are liable to change

ARROW BOOKS, BOOKSERVICE BY POST, PO BOX 29, DOUGLAS, ISLE
OF MAN, BRITISH ISLES

NAME..

ADDRESS...

....

....

Please enclose a cheque or postal order made out to Arrow Books Ltd. for the amount
due and allow the following for postage and packing.

U.K. CUSTOMERS: Please allow 22p per book to a maximum of £3.00.

B.F.P.O. & EIRE: Please allow 22p per book to a maximum of £3.00.

OVERSEAS CUSTOMERS: Please allow 22p per book.

Whilst every effort is made to keep prices low it is sometimes necessary to increase cover
prices at short notice. Arrow Books reserve the right to show new retail prices on covers
which may differ from those previously advertised in the text or elsewhere.

Bestselling Non-Fiction

☐	Complete Hip and Thigh Diet	Rosemary Conley	£2.99
☐	Staying off the Beaten Track	Elizabeth Gundrey	£6.99
☐	Raw Energy: Recipes	Leslie Kenton	£3.99
☐	The PM System	Dr J A Muir Gray	£5.99
☐	Women Who Love Too Much	Robin Norwood	£3.50
☐	Letters From Women Who Love Too Much	Robin Norwood	£3.50
☐	Fat is a Feminist Issue	Susie Orbach	£2.99
☐	Callanetics	Callan Pinckney	£6.99
☐	Elvis and Me	Priscilla Presley	£3.50
☐	Love, Medicine and Miracles	Bernie Siegel	£3.50
☐	Communion	Whitley Strieber	£3.50
☐	Trump: The Art of the Deal	Donald Trump	£3.99

Prices and other details are liable to change

Bestselling General Fiction

☐ No Enemy But Time	Evelyn Anthony	£2.95
☐ Skydancer	Geoffrey Archer	£3.50
☐ The Sisters	Pat Booth	£3.50
☐ Captives of Time	Malcolm Bosse	£2.99
☐ Saudi	Laurie Devine	£2.95
☐ Duncton Wood	William Horwood	£4.50
☐ Aztec	Gary Jennings	£3.95
☐ A World Apart	Marie Joseph	£3.50
☐ The Ladies of Missalonghi	Colleen McCullough	£2.50
☐ Lily Golightly	Pamela Oldfield	£3.50
☐ Sarum	Edward Rutherfurd	£4.99
☐ Communion	Whitley Strieber	£3.99

Prices and other details are liable to change

ARROW BOOKS, BOOKSERVICE BY POST, PO BOX 29, DOUGLAS, ISLE OF MAN, BRITISH ISLES

NAME...

ADDRESS...

....

....

Please enclose a cheque or postal order made out to Arrow Books Ltd. for the amount due and allow the following for postage and packing.

U.K. CUSTOMERS: Please allow 22p per book to a maximum of £3.00.

B.F.P.O. & EIRE: Please allow 22p per book to a maximum of £3.00.

OVERSEAS CUSTOMERS: Please allow 22p per book.

Whilst every effort is made to keep prices low it is sometimes necessary to increase cover prices at short notice. Arrow Books reserve the right to show new retail prices on covers which may differ from those previously advertised in the text or elsewhere.

Arrow Health

☐ The Alexander Principle	Wilfred Barlow	£2.95
☐ The Zinc Solution	D. Bryce-Smith	£3.50
☐ Goodbye to Arthritis	Patricia Byrivers	£2.95
☐ Rosemary Conley's Complete Hip and Thigh Diet	Rosemary Conley	£2.99
☐ No Change	Wendy Cooper	£2.99
☐ Day Light Robbery	Dr Damien Downing	£3.99
☐ The Biogenic Diet	Leslie Kenton	£3.99
☐ Ageless Ageing: The Natural Way to Stay Young	Leslie Kenton	£3.95
☐ Raw Energy: Recipes	Leslie Kenton	£3.99
☐ Joy of Beauty	Leslie Kenton	£6.99
☐ Sexual Cystitis	Angela Kilmartin	£3.99
☐ PM System: Preventive Medicine For Total Health	Dr JA Muir Gray	£5.99
☐ Women Who Love Too Much	Robin Norwood	£3.50
☐ Fat is a Feminist Issue	Susie Orbach	£2.99
☐ Callanetics	Callan Pinckney	£6.99
☐ Love, Medicine and Miracles	Bernie Siegel	£3.50

Prices and other details are liable to change

ARROW BOOKS, BOOKSERVICE BY POST, PO BOX 29, DOUGLAS, ISLE
OF MAN, BRITISH ISLES

NAME..

ADDRESS...

....

....

Please enclose a cheque or postal order made out to Arrow Books Ltd. for the amount
due and allow the following for postage and packing.

U.K. CUSTOMERS: Please allow 22p per book to a maximum of £3.00.

B.F.P.O. & EIRE: Please allow 22p per book to a maximum of £3.00.

OVERSEAS CUSTOMERS: Please allow 22p per book.

Whilst every effort is made to keep prices low it is sometimes necessary to increase cover
prices at short notice. Arrow Books reserve the right to show new retail prices on covers
which may differ from those previously advertised in the text or elsewhere.